Beyond Amelia:
Lesser-known Women of Yesteryear

L. B. Hillsinger

Introduction: The March of History

The march of history has often been taught through what historians call the "big man" approach: the generals, the presidents, the dictators, the adventurers, and the scientists that changed the course of history. A handful of the "big men" of history have been women, Cleopatra, Marie Curie, and Amelia Earhart, to name a few.

Historians also teach history through the lives of ordinary people, how the lives of the common soldier, the farmer, or the shopkeeper changed because a war broke out, a new king was crowned, or someone invented a new and better "mousetrap." However, the lives of ordinary people rarely make history. When a war breaks out, a king imposes new taxes, or when automobiles replace horses, ordinary people are swept up in the march of history. Except for the occasional hero, ordinary people are not history-makers.

Between the "big names" of history and ordinary people lie the lesser-known names of history. For each "big name" in history, there are hundreds, if not thousands, of minor names. Arguably, as there are so many more minor figures in history than "big names," the minor figures have affected the march of history more than the "big names." Lesser-known names like Nellie Ross, who, in 1925, served as the first female governor, or Margret Knight, who invented the modern paper bag. Or Anne Connelly, who invited the first fire escape system. Or Maria Bealey, who invented the modern life raft, or Mary Anderson, who invented wiper blades. Or Lizzie Magie, who developed *The Landlords' Game*, a precursor to the game of Monopoly.

An old-fashioned saying claims, "Behind every good man is a good woman." The reverse is also true. Often, "the good man" behind "the good woman" was her father. Around 2,300 B.C. King Sargon appointed his daughter, Enheduanna, as high priestess. As the high priestess, Enheduanna wrote poetry, hymns, and essays. Enheduanna is widely considered to be the first identified author in history.

Sometimes the "good man" is the woman's husband. Most people have never heard of George Putnam. However, his wife, Amelia Earhart, is certainly a "big name" in history. George Putnam not only supported and helped finance his wife's aviation pursuits. He supported Amelia's ill-fated circumnavigation of the globe with another man, Amelia's navigator, Fred Noonan.

Most collections of biographies of women of history focus on a specific time (e.g., women of the 19th century) or groups (e.g., women of science). *Beyond Amelia* takes a broader approach. Some women profiled here are "big names" in their own culture but are largely unknown in the west. It was felt that by casting a wider net and not focusing on one particular time period or occupation, a broader truth would emerge.

Five types of interesting but lesser-known women of yesteryear are profiled: Adventurers, entrepreneurs, queens (both literal and figurative), scientists and scholars, and spies. As we shall see, the influence of fathers, husbands, and other men differed whether the woman was an adventurer, an entrepreneur, a queen, a scientist, or a spy.

Each chapter is arranged chronologically. Most chapters begin in the 17th century and conclude just after WWII.

Beyond Amelia is not intended as a scholarly analysis. It is intended to be an easy yet informative read. Still, when warranted, assumptions others have made about historical events have been challenged. Also, when the historical record is vague, plausible explanations for events have been offered and are labeled as such.

Enjoy.

L. B. Hillsinger

San Luis Obispo, California

2023

ADVENTURERS

Introduction:

In yesteryear, most men, and certainly most women in their lifetimes, never traveled more than twenty-five miles from home. A man who craved excitement and adventure could join his nation's army or navy. Life as a common soldier or sailor was not easy, but for many, the thrill of adventure outweighed any hardships. While a career as a soldier or sailor promised adventure (and hardship), the pay was usually modest. A potentially more lucrative and exciting "profession" was that of a pirate.

Piracy is as old as sailing. In the third century B.C., for decades, Teuta and her armada harassed Roman shipping. In the history of Caribbean piracy, only two female pirates, Anny Bonny and Mary Read, are well known. In the South China Sea, in the 18th century, Zheng Yi Sao commanded the largest pirate fleet ever. Her exploits are well known in Asia.

With the Industrial Revolution of the 19th century, railroads connected major cities, and steamships replaced sailing ships. Traveling to see distant new lands meant months, not years. Adventure travel was possible. Capitalizing on the notion of (relatively) easy travel, Jules Verne wrote his classic *Around the World in 80 Days*. In a not-so-friendly competition, two businessmen financed the adventure of two women, Nellie Bly, and Elizabeth Bisland, to race around the world.

In the early 20th century, the Wright Brothers invented the airplane, and just a decade later, the first commercial air service began. As a nod to Amelia Earhart, we'll take a look at the life of Ruth Law. In 1917, Ruth shattered the previous record for the longest-powered flight.

Finally, we will conclude this section with Elizabeth Bell. By age 21, Elizabeth traveled more than most people in the 21st century. Among other modes of transportation, she used one of the oldest—the camel.

Anne Bonny and Mary Read

Anne Bonny and Mary Read were born at the height of the Golden Age of Piracy, an era where pirates plundered all types of cargo but especially gold. Gold that had been plundered out of the New World. The deaths of Anny Bonny and Mary Read and the death of their shipmates, arguably mark the beginning in the final chapter of the Golden Age of Piracy.

Piracy in the Caribbean had a unique set of rules. In battles, the captain's orders were to be followed without question. However, outside of battle, decisions were made by consensus, and by a vote of the crew, a captain could be relieved of his duties. Further, unlike on a naval vessel, members of the crew were free to leave the ship at any friendly harbor. Pirate ships in the Caribbean were multi-cultural. Sailing skills were far more important than nationality or race. Given the democratic nature of piracy in the Caribbean, a pirate fleet rarely constituted more than a few ships.

As a ship's captain could get voted out of his position, pirate captains treated their crew much better than captains on military ships. On a military ship, discipline was harsh and flogging common. Flogging was not banned on US ships until 1850 and was not completely banned in the British navy flogging until 1881. Further, for very serious offenses, on a naval vessel, a sailor could be keel-hauled, literally dragging the offender under the keel—a punishment that usually, but not always, resulted in death. Given the harsh discipline on naval vessels and the potential for substantial reward, a "career" as a pirate made sense to many.

Unlike serving in the navy, a pirate could dress however he (or she wanted). Pirates often sported a gold (or brass) earring on one ear. According to legend, if a pirate died, the earring was for payment for a decent burial. History does not record exactly how Anne Bonny or Mary Read dressed, but history does record that they dressed as pirates and not as fashionable women.

Falling between military service as a sailor and the free spirit of being a pirate was being a privateer. Captains of privateer vessels were issued "Letters of Marque" from a national government. With a Letter of Marque, a sea captain, as a privateer, was authorized to plunder ships from a specific country.

However, in practice, if an opportunity arose, privateers plundered ships from any country except their own.

The authority of congress to grant Letters of Marquee is expressly in the constitution. In the War of 1812, congress granted approximately five hundred letters of Marquee. Letters of Marquee have since been banned by international treaty, but that didn't stop Congressman Ron Paul in 2009 from suggesting that letters of Marque be issued to deal with the pirates off the Somali coast.

Many historians have claimed that there was little difference between pirates and privateers. For cargo, this is correct. Cargo, whether seized by pirates or privateers, is the same loss. However, on a naval warship, if given the opportunity, a sailor could defect and become a pirate. (It never worked the other way). However, a French sailor would never defect to a British or Spanish privateer or vice versa. Mary Read served on a military vessel before becoming a pirate. Anne Bonny went into piracy from the start.

Some sources say Anne Bonny was born in 1695. Others say she was born in 1698. Many, but not all sources, say that Anne's father was a man by the name of William Cormac and that Anne's mother was a servant in Cormac's home. According to most, at some time in the early 1700s, William Cormac, his wife, Anne's mother (the servant), and Anne sailed from Ireland and settled in what was then known as Charles Town, Carolina.

Charles Town, like many towns along the Eastern seaboard at the time, was struggling financially. Initially, pirates coming into town were actually welcomed. Pirates buying provisions, drinking at taverns, visiting the local brothels, etc., brought in much-needed income. However, as cities prospered, residents' attitudes toward pirates changed. Shipping goods without fear became more important than pirates splurging their money about town.

In Charles Town, Anne married a local pirate named James Bonny. Anne's father was willing to do business with pirates, but his daughter marrying a pirate was unacceptable. However, Cormac could not stop the marriage, and Anne and James married. Anne and James made their home in Nassau. In his definitive book on piracy, Colin Woodward considers the Bahamas the "Republic of Pirates" as a formal government barely existed. According to Woodward and others, Anne became Nassau's "most infamous harlot."

One of the better-known pirates in the Bahamas and throughout the Caribbean was John "Calico Jack" Rackham. By the time Anne Bonny made her home in Nassau, Mary Read was already a part of Calico Jack's crew. Mary Read was born in 1685, making her ten (or seven) years older than Anne. Before Mary was born, her mother had married a sailor. They had one child, a boy; however, he died quite young. She hid the child's death from the paternal side of the family.

While her husband was at sea, Mary's mother had an extra-marital affair and became pregnant with Mary. During the pregnancy, Mary's mother learned that her husband had died. For financial support, the widow turned to her mother-in-law. She disguised Mary as her late (half)brother. To maintain the ruse, her mother dressed Mary as a boy. This continued through her childhood. If town folk learned Mary was a girl, presumably, the grandmother would learn the truth and cut off any financial support.

In her late teens or early 20s, disguised as a man, Mary joined the British Navy. She saw action against the French. While in the navy, Mary met and married a Flemish (modern-day Belgian) man. How Mary's future husband learned of her true gender does not appear to be recorded.

After concluding their military service, Mary and her husband owned and operated an inn. A few years later, however, Mary's husband died. Mary could have continued running the inn, but she wanted to return to the adventure that could be found at sea. Disguised as a man, she joined Dutch Navy. However, Mary resigned her commission and sailed, as a civilian, to the West Indies. Some sources report that she had remarried.

According to the website Historic UK, the man Mary married was a pirate. Historic UK further reports that Mary's new husband got into a conflict with another pirate. A land-based duel with swords was scheduled to settle the dispute. When Mary learned of the duel and, knowing she was better with a sword than her husband, she set a duel with the aggrieved pirate. They set their duel two hours before her husband's duel. In this tale, Mary slew the other pirate and saved her husband's life.

However, most sources do not report such a duel. Further, in the democracy that was piracy, such an encounter was uncommon. Moreover, it would have been foolhardy for the aggrieved pirate to accept back-to-back duels. The tale of Mary chivalrously dueling another pirate to save her husband's life is likely simple embellishment.

Sources agree that Mary defected to the pirate cause and joined Calico Jack's crew. For Calico Jack and many pirates, Nassau was basecamp. The largest town in the Bahamas, Nassau, was still more of a town than a city. Given Nassau's small population, it was inevitable that Anne Bonny, Calico Jack, and Mary Read would become acquainted.

At some point, Calico Jack, and Anne became smitten with each other. Some sources say that Mary was attracted to Anne (while dressed as a man) and that Mary only learned that Anne was a woman after Calico Jack told her. Calico Jack's reported jealousy of Anne's attraction to Mary may have reflected a prior romantic relationship between Calico Jack and Mary. While Calico Jack may have had a romantic relationship with Anne (or both women) in an era when having a woman on board was considered bad luck, he accepted Anne and Mary as members of the crew.

In January 1718, the British government appointed a man named Woodes Rogers, governor of the Bahamas. Rogers' mandate was to restore British authority over the island. The contingent of soldiers Rogers brought with him was large enough to show that Britain meant business but not enough to fully overwhelm the pirates (nor the Spanish some years later). To avoid bloodshed and because it was cheaper in men and ships, Rogers offered pardons to the pirates. Many small-time pirates accepted the offer. Whether James Bonny did so is not clear. Calico Jack clearly did not.

Calico Jack still wanted the life of a pirate and wanted Anne to join him. He asked James Bonny to annul his marriage to Anne. Given Anne's reputation around town, James had good reason to agree. Likely because he felt intimidated by his wife's pirate-lover, Bonny agreed to annul the marriage and even gave the new couple a substantial sum of money.

Calico Jack and Anne Bonny needed a witness to certify the annulment. They found a witness by the name of Richard Turley. It proved to be a poor choice, as Richard Turley informed Governor Rogers of the request for annulment. Rogers, as governor, had the final say in all legal matters, including divorce, on the island.

Rogers refused to grant the annulment. Further, he said that if he could, he would imprison Anne and whip her until she promised to keep "loose company no more." Anne skipped the formalities of an annulment and joined up with Calico Jack.

Hollywood, as is often the case, has taken great liberties with the story of Anne Bonny. In the *Black Sails* series, Anne's husband, James Bonny, is depicted as an abusive husband who pimped out his underage wife, Anne, to sailors, including Calico Jack. In truth, Anne openly cheated on her husband, and it was Governor Rogers who threatened violence. Further, the historical record is clear that Anne joined up with Calico Jack of her own free will.

Sensing that it was best to put some distance between themselves and Governor Rodgers, on August 12, 1720, Calico Jack, Anne Bonny, Mary Read, and six other pirates stole a six-gun sloop, *The William,* and sailed out of Nassau. They plundered fishing boats and other lower-value targets, but real plunder proved elusive. Then they came upon Richard Turley, who had ratted them out to the governor. They threatened to whip him if they ever found him again. To back up their threat, they destroyed his boat.

Perhaps reasoning if they could not find merchant ships carrying plunder, the crew decided attacking privateers might be more successful. Calico Jack and crew found and attacked a privateer captained by Jean Bondavaris. However, Bondavaris successfully retreated. Bondavaris contacted a fellow privateer by the name of Jonathan Barnet. Barnet had a well-armed sloop and was already looking for Calico Jack. Barnet successfully pursued Calico Jack and ordered him to surrender.

Most sources say that except for Anne and Mary, the Calico's Jack crew had been drinking heavily and remained below deck while Anne Bonny and Mary Read valiantly remained topside, ready to defend the ship. Hoping to avoid battle, capture the boat and the crew, Barnet's ship fired a swivel gun, a type of gun used for signaling, not actual combat, at Calico Jack's sloop. Someone in the Calico Jack's crew yelled they would not surrender.

Barnet's men attacked with cannon. The boom and the mainsail of *The William* sustained heavy damage. Calico Jack's crew then pleaded for "quarter" (meaning they desired mercy and would not resist any further). The entire crew, including Anne Bonny and Mary Read, went to Nassau to stand trial. The standard sentence for piracy was death by hanging.

Trials on charges of piracy had a modicum of due process. If the accused was especially young or forced by circumstances to join the pirate cause, an acquittal was possible. However, there was no doubt about Calico Jack's guilt or that of the other men. They allowed Calico Jack to visit Anne before his appointment with the gallows.

Anne and Mary's trial began on November 28, 1720. Many witnessing the trial probably assumed Anne and Mary were captives and victims—not pirates. However, multiple witnesses reported that Anne Bonny and Mary Read were true pirates. The judge had no choice but to find Anne and Mary guilty of piracy and ordered them hanged. However, Anne and Mary informed the judge they were, in the language of the day, "with child." The judge postponed their death sentences.

The father of Anne's child clearly was Calico Jack. But what about Mary? Who was the father of her child? As noted, she may or may not have married a pirate. However, even if she had married, she likely separated from her husband well before joining up with Calico Jack. Was Calico Jack or another crew member the father? Did Mary even know who the father was?

If Anne and Mary knew they were pregnant at trial, and the trial occurred only weeks after their capture, Anne and Mary likely already knew they were pregnant at the time of their capture. While Fetal Alcohol Syndrome would not be a diagnosis for centuries, even in the early 18th century, a pregnant woman would be expected to moderate her drinking. Anne and Mary may have been sober and ready to defend the ship because they knew they were pregnant.

Likely due to a fever, Mary Read died in prison in late April 1721. Unless she had a miscarriage, she was at least seven months pregnant when she died. The exact date of her death is not recorded, suggesting a lapse in supervision by her jailers. Her burial on April 28, 1721, however, is well-documented.

What happened to Anne Bonny and her child is less clear. Many sources say her father intervened and returned Anne to the American colonies. Some sources say Anne married, had several children, and died in her eighties. However, a woman named Ann Bonny is listed in the ledger of deaths for St. Catherine's Parish in Jamaica. In the 1700s, Ann was usually spelled without an "e" at the end. The "e" was added by historical convention. Given Nassau's small population, the chances that there was another Ann Bonny were quite slim.

The date of death given for Ann Bonny is listed in the church ledger as December 29, 1733. If this is correct, Anne Bonny served thirteen years in prison before she died. There is no baptismal, birth, or other record of her child, so Anne Bonny likely miscarried while in prison.

Given the jail conditions in the 18th century, the primitive medical care existing then, and the often oppressive heat of the Caribbean, it is likely that both Mary and Anne miscarried while in prison and later died while incarcerated. For them, the adventuresome life of a pirate came at a high cost.

Zheng Yi Sao

In the late 18th and early 19th centuries, America had its own problem with pirates. Pirates based on the northwest coast of Africa terrorized American and European vessels. As these pirates acted with the authority of local sultans, technically, they were privateers, but by historical convention, history refers to them as the Barbary pirates. After a while, the Barbary pirates realized there was an easier way of plundering. Instead of seizing vessels and risking the loss of life, it was easier to demand tribute (protection money) to allow safe passage.

Unlike the other national powers, America decided not to pay. This was a bold decision for a young country. Raising a navy would be expensive. Also, there were fears that a standing navy would give the President as "commander-in-chief" too much power. Still, a navy was raised, and after several battles and skirmishes, the United States successfully defeated the pirates. This victory is celebrated in the line "from the shores of Tripoli" in the Marine Hymn.

At about the same time, on the other side of the world, Zhang Yi Sao, like the Barbary Pirates, demanded protection money for safe passage. Born Shin Yang in 1775, Zheng Yi Sao would lead, in sheer numbers, the largest fleet ever assembled.

Most sources report that, as a young woman, Shin Yang worked as a prostitute, or more likely, a Madame of her own brothel. Exactly when Shin Yan met her future husband, Zhang Yi, is unclear. As a Madame of a brothel, Shin Yang may have known about the plans of customers. This could be why Zheng Yi sought her out. Whatever the initial motivation, in 1801, Shin Yang and Zheng Yi married. Shin Yang then became known as Zheng Yi Sao or the wife of Zheng Yi.

Before his marriage to Shin Yang, Zheng Yi had organized disparate pirate forces into a single force. The entire armada consisted of 1500 ships and approximately 150,000 men. By comparison, the Spanish Armada had 150 ships, 8,000 sailors, and 30,000 troops. As Pirate-Commander-In-Chief, Zheng Yi established a system where the collective plunder was diligently and fairly distributed.

Around 1798 and three years before his marriage to Shin Yang, Zheng Yi had taken a fifteen-year-old Vietnamese boy named Cheung Po into his crew, possibly adopting the young man. Why did Zheng Yi take on a Vietnamese teenager and give him responsibilities beyond his years? Your author speculates that it might have been a strategic decision. Just as kings married off daughters to keep peace with a rival kingdom, taking Cheung Po under his wing, whether Cheung Po wanted to or not, may have been a means for Zheng Yi to cement his ties with Vietnamese authorities. Zheng Yi didn't want to be pursued by both Chinese and Vietnamese. Whether officially adopted or not, it is clear that Cheung Po was given responsibilities beyond more senior sailors. When she married Cheung Po's boss, Zheng Yi Sao was just twenty-six years old and just six years older than Cheung Po.

At his new wife's urging, Zheng Yi erected a giant floating pagoda. The priests tending to the pagoda were, of course, on Zheng Yi's payroll. Before a battle, the priests offered prayers. As Zheng Yi was so successful, his leadership took on an aura of divine intervention. The aura of divine intervention was made possible because Zheng Yi accepted his wife's proposal to build a pagoda. Divine intervention, however, didn't protect Zheng Yi for long. He died in 1807, just four years after his marriage to Shin Yang.

Most sources say Zheng Yi died of drowning after falling overboard. However, as an experienced sea captain, it is highly unlikely that Zheng fell overboard of his accord. He may have been pushed overboard by his protégé Cheung Po or Zheng Yi Yao, or both. Whether they were accomplices in the murder, if not already, they became lovers.

Despite Zheng Yi's death by accident or design, someone needed to assume command of the armada. Cheung Po, as the second in command, was one potential choice. However, Cheung Po was Vietnamese and having him as captain would bring complications. With the backing of Cheung Po and other officers, Zheng Yi Sao assumed command of the armada.

As admiral of the large armada, Zheng Li Sao is credited with establishing a formal set of rules regarding discipline. For instance, unauthorized shore leave would result in an ear being cut off. More serious offenses, like willful disobedience or stealing from the collective plunder, meant death. Death was also the punishment for raping a female prisoner or having sex with a captive woman—even if she did the seducing. (To gain some favor or even release, a female captive might try seduction). However, the rules allowed for romance. A crew member could marry a captive woman and leave the ship.

An armada of 1500 ships can't rely on the income of plunder alone. Under her leadership, Zheng Yi Sao's forces engaged in extortion. Like the Barbary Pirates, tribute was demanded to ensure safe passage through their territory. Zheng Yi Sao went one step further; like a mafia don, Zheng Yi Sao controlled the docks. Merchants who needed to transport their goods had to pay protection money. In particular, Zheng Yi Sao had a complete lock on the salt trade. In an era before refrigeration, salt was critical as a preservative.

As a "mafia don," Zheng Yi Sao's authority was so strong that her crews didn't even have to enter ports to intimidate merchants. She established an office in Macao where merchants could conveniently submit protection payments. Zheng Yi Sao also had numerous government officials on her payroll. The Chinese military was far too weak to take on Zheng Yi Sao. She wielded more power than the Barbary pirates.

China sought help from the Western powers, the British, the Dutch, and the Portuguese, to subdue Zheng Yi Sao. There were several battles, but Zheng Yi Sao's well-trained, well-disciplined armada held its own against the greatest navies in the world. Still, many lives on both sides were lost.

Like the British in the Caribbean, to avoid further losses in men and ships, Chinese authorities offered Zheng Yi Sao and other pirates, pardons. Zheng Yi Sao and much of her crew accepted.

Some sources say that Cheung Po reneged on his promise and returned to piracy. Whether Cheung Po continued in piracy, returned to Vietnam, joined the Chinese navy, or pursued another path, he and Zheng Yi Sao parted ways.

Permanently back onshore and flush with ill-gotten gains, Zheng Yi Sao opened a brothel and a gambling hall. She became a mother and grandmother. She died in 1844 at the age of sixty-six.

Nellie Bly and Elizabeth Bisland

By the late 19th century, telegraph service connected the major cities of North America and Europe. With telegraph service, newspapers could report on national and international events in near real-time. The adventures of Nellie Bly and Elizabeth Bisland became the newspaper equivalent of a modern viral video.

Inspired by Jules Verne's Around the World in 80 Days, Joseph Pulitzer, for whom the Pulitzer award is named, sponsored Nelly Bly to circumnavigate the globe. Accounts differ about who approached whom with the idea. However, his paper, The New York World, bankrolled Nelly's trip around the globe. Of course, this was not a paid vacation. Pulitzer expected Nellie to send dispatches of her travels, making readers eager to buy the New York World.

Pulitzer had good reason to be confident in Nellie. Nellie had already captured the nation's attention with her expose of New York City's treatment of the mentally ill. She had faked being mentally ill and got herself admitted to Bellevue Hospital. After her release, Nellie chronicled the mistreatment of the mentally ill in a series of newspaper articles. The articles turned into a bestseller, *Ten Days in a Madhouse,* and spurned major reforms in the care for the mentally ill.

On November 14, 1989, Nellie left for her trip around the world from Hoboken, New Jersey. Her departure, of course, was front-page news. In Nellie's day, women rarely traveled alone. Women who traveled did so with their husbands and typically brought multiple bags. If a porter or bellman wasn't available, her husband carried the bags. To show that a woman didn't need to travel with an extensive wardrobe, Nellie took minimal luggage. As an aside, when luggage with wheels became commercially available in the 1970s, acceptance was slow; men did not want to look weak by wheeling luggage.

Like almost everyone else in America, John Brisbane Walker, the publisher of Cosmopolitan magazine, learned of Nellie's quest in the daily newspaper. Walker realized there would be enormous publicity if another woman were to race Nellie around the world. Walker knew what woman he wanted for the job, his literary editor, Elizabeth Bisland. Elizabeth spoke French and was also exceptionally beautiful. In short, Elizabeth was "sophisticated and cultured," an adjective few would pin on Nellie.

Walker, like Pulitzer, was taking a risk. If one or both women received serious injuries, were mugged, raped, murdered, or simply disappeared, readers would turn on the men. They would get the blame for sending women—alone—on an obviously dangerous quest dreamed up by a French novelist.

Elizabeth initially rejected Walker's proposal. She told her boss she had friends coming over for dinner the next day and did not want to cancel. She also didn't want the notoriety such a trip would bring. Walker, however, would not be easily dissuaded. He offered Elizabeth a financial deal that was too good to give up. Reportedly, he also threatened to fire her if she didn't take the assignment. Elizabeth was twenty-eight years old and, like twenty-five-year-old Nellie, unmarried. When Elizabeth departed westward, Nellie had a seventeen-hour head start, and was going eastward to Europe.

In France, Nellie met briefly with Jules Verne, whose novel had inspired her trip. She continued east, through the Suez Canal, then to Sri Lanka, then known as Ceylon, and Hong Kong. It wasn't until Nellie reached Hong Kong that Nellie learned of Elizabeth's trip. However, Nellie downplayed the importance of who would return home first.

Still, being first was important to Pulitzer and Bisland. Coming in second would not boost readership; only coming in first would help the bottom line. Which was the entire purpose in funding the adventure. To garner more publicity, Pulitzer ran a contest where readers could guess the day and time of Nellie's arrival. Further, to help Nellie win, Pulitzer arranged for a private train for the final leg of the trip from San Francisco to New Jersey. There is also evidence that Pulitzer's agents may have misled Elizabeth about her ship's departure, causing a two-day delay in her departure. Nellie completed her journey in seventy-two days. Elizabeth's trip took seventy-six days.

Both women penned books about their trips. Capitalizing on Jules Verne Nellie titled her book, *Around the World in Seventy-Two Days*. Elizabeth titled hers *In Seven Stages: A Flying Trip Around The World,* a rather odd title, as the Wright Brothers would not take flight for another twelve years.

Elizabeth was the first to get married. In 1891, she married Charles Wetmore, a lawyer. Using her maiden name, she continued her literary writing.

Elizabeth's marriage to Charles did not produce any children. Elizabeth's last book, *Three Wise Men,* was published posthumously in 1930.

In 1895, Nellie married industrialist Robert Seaman. She was thirty-one years old. He was seventy-three. Seaman is credited with the creation of the fifty-five-gallon barrel of oil, a standard still used today. Nellie received two patents of her own, one for a special type of commercial milk can and another for stackable garbage bins.

In 1904, Robert died. While Nellie had many skills, she was not a good business manager. The company she inherited from her husband went bankrupt.

As a widow, Nellie returned to doing what she knew best: journalism. When WWI broke out, Nellie was one of the few female war correspondents. She was the only journalist to cover action along the Austria/Serbia border and was briefly detained as a suspected spy for the British.

Nellie died in 1922. She was buried at the Woodlawn Cemetery in the Bronx. Elizabeth died seven years later. By sheer coincidence, she was also buried at Woodlawn Cemetery. The two likely never met in person.

Ruth Law

Ruth Law was born on May 21, 1887. She was one year old when Edison invented the first motion picture camera. Her older brother, Rodman, became one of the first stuntmen in the silent picture industry. While older brothers are often competitive with their younger brothers, most do not challenge their younger sisters in competitive play. Rodman was different; he challenged his sister to keep up with him. If Rodman had treated Ruth like most brothers at the time treated their younger sisters, Ruth might not have gained the confidence to become a pilot.

Ruth was sixteen when the Wright Brothers took their first flight. Ruth asked Orville Wright to give her flying lessons but saying that women didn't have the mechanical inclination to fly an airplane, Orville refused. Ruth then found two ahead-of-their-times men, Harry Atwood, and Arch Freeman, to give her flying lessons. In 1912, eleven years before Amelia Earhart, Ruth earned her pilot's license.

Ruth earned money doing airshows. In 1915, Ruth stunned a crowd by doing not one but two loop-the-loops, a feat few other pilots had accomplished. According to the NASM (National Academy of Sports Medicine) website, Ruth earned as much as $9,000 a week ($250,000 in 2020 dollars). However, this is likely an exaggeration. Typically, air shows garnered, at best, several thousand spectators. At fifty cents a ticket (ten times the cost of a movie at the time) to net $9,000, Ruth would have needed 18,000 paying spectators—before expenses.

While the stunts impressed crowds, most men (and certainly most women) were afraid to fly. Flying was also expensive and far more expensive than traveling by train. To be commercially successful, airlines needed businessmen to overcome their fears of flying and book tickets. On ships, stewards tended to passengers. To attract business travelers (who were almost exclusively male), airlines intentionally hired women as stewardesses; if women could fly, so could men.

While airlines struggled to woo wary passengers, professional baseball also struggled financially. Baseball club owners relied on attendance, not ad revenue, to pay players' salaries. An empty ballpark was bad for the bottom line.

To promote professional baseball, Ruth agreed to do a stunt with Casey Stengel, a popular player. In the stunt, Casey was supposed to drop a baseball from the airplane, and Wilbert Robinson, a former player, was supposed to catch it. However, someone forgot to bring a baseball, so Casey improvised with a grapefruit instead. The grapefruit knocked Robinson off his feet, and the local baseball league became nicknamed "The Grapefruit League."

Two years later, Ruth truly redeemed herself. She flew nonstop for 452 miles from Chicago to upstate New York, shattering the previous distance record. Shortly afterward, Ruth triumphantly flew around the Statue of Liberty. Some sources say she spelled out L-I-B-E-R-T-Y in Morse code. This is most likely an embellishment. Ruth's plane was an older model, and "running lights" on planes were not yet common. Other sources say she used flares to spell out L-I-B-E-R-I-T-Y. That is clearly an exaggeration. Doing so would have required an inordinate number of flares and superhuman timing in lighting and dropping the flares. Whatever the truth, if any, to the Morse Code story, a few days after her flight around the Statue of Liberty, Ruth met with President Wilson and other dignitaries

WWI broke out two years later. Ruth tried to enlist in the fledging US Army Air Corp but was not allowed to do so. She did get to wear a uniform. Some sources say she was authorized to drop leaflets over enemy territory but was not approved to engage other planes or shoot at troops on the ground. Sanctioning a pilot to fly into enemy territory without authorization to shoot would seem to put the pilot at even greater risk.

However, in WWI, there was still some chivalry in warfare. This chivalry was not based on gender, as unless she flew extremely low, troops assume a man was the pilot. Rather, the chivalry was based on fairness. For instance, shooting an unarmed soldier on the ground would be unfair. Similarly, in WWI, submarine commanders often allowed an enemy crew to man lifeboats before torpedoing their vessel. Still, flying itself was dangerous. In WWI, the fatality rate for WWI pilots from accidents was significantly greater than that from combat. Sources agree that Ruth's greatest contribution to the war was teaching other pilots how to fly. Her notoriety was also used to sell war bonds.

After the war, Ruth and her husband, Charles Oliver, formed "Ruth's Flying Circus." Two other (male) pilots were part of their air show, but Ruth was the draw for the crowd. Outside of stunt flying, Ruth flew a record 14,000 feet in altitude, but the record didn't hold long. In modern aviation, continuous supplemental oxygen is required above 14,000.

Ruth's husband, however, became increasingly concerned that fate would catch up with his wife. In 1922, without telling Ruth, Charles took out an ad announcing Ruth's retirement. Publicly Ruth said it was a good time to retire as aviation stunts were getting riskier and riskier. She added, "It's my husband's turn now; I've been in the limelight long enough." One wonders what she told her husband in private.

Ruth sold her plane and most of her other aviation equipment. She and her husband settled in Beverly Hills. They lived there for several years, then moved to San Francisco. The year after they moved, Charles died. Like Nelly and Elizabeth, Ruth had no children.

In 1948, Ruth attended an event at the Smithsonian celebrating the Wright Brothers' first flight. Multiple sources noted she traveled to the event by train, implying that she did not wish to fly. However, traveling by airplane was still quite expensive. The decision to take the train could have been merely financial.

Ruth died in 1970 at the age of 70. Three years later, the first woman captained a commercial flight on a major airline.

Gertrude Bell

Gertrude Bell was born in Durham, England, on July 14, 1868. Gertrude was born in the era when the sun never set on the British Empire, and The Empire was still largely intact when she died.

Gertrude's father was a businessman who held progressive views. Unlike many other industrialists in the 19th Century, Gertrude's father paid his employees decently and treated them well.

Gertrude's grandfather was a member of parliament, and her uncle was an ambassador to Persia (modern-day Iran). Her father's progressive views, and her uncle's worldliness helped shaped who she became.

When Gertrude was three years old, her mother died in childbirth. Her father remarried when Gertrude was seven years old. Gertrude's stepmother was a playwright and wrote children's stories. She also penned an article about her husband's progressive business practices.

Gertrude attended college at Queen's College and Oxford. Her major was modern history. Gertrude was the first woman to earn a degree with such a major. After graduating, Gertrude went to Persia to visit her uncle. She recounted her trip to Persia in her first book, *Persian Pictures*. Gertrude became fluent in Persian (Farsi), as well as Arabic. From her subsequent travels in Syria came a second book, *The Desert and the Sown*.

In 1907, Gertrude teamed up with archeologist Sir Willman M. Ramsay and cataloged ruins in Turkey. The two partnered up to write what we call today a "coffee-table book," *A Thousand and One Churches*. In 1913, on another excursion to the region, Gertrude was held hostage for several days.

Besides having a fondness for Middle Eastern Culture and being an amateur archaeologist, Gertrude loved mountain climbing. In 1902, she attempted to climb Finsteraarhorn, a mountain just over 14,000 feet in elevation. The hiking party, however, became caught in a blizzard. They had to wait out the storm for over fifty hours. Gertrude suffered frost-bitten hands and feet. Despite this harrowing experience, she climbed the Matterhorn the next year.

While mountain climbing was recreational, Gertrude's second home was, as it was called then, the Near East. The term the Middle East is a modern invention. The designation came into use because the Suez Canal is roughly at the midpoint between shipping routes from Britain to India.

Gertrude traveled extensively throughout the Arab world. Westerners, then, as well as today, often see "Arabs" or "Muslims" together as a monolithic group; Gertrude, however, learned the local politics. She learned the lay of the land both figuratively and literally. She often wrote letters home about her travels and the people she met. Posthumously, her stepmother published a compilation of these letters.

Before WWI, Egypt was nominally part of the Ottoman Empire, and predominately Sunni Muslim. The Caliph, the religious leader of Sunni Muslims, lived in Turkey, the seat of the Ottoman Empire. However, with the building of the Suez Canal, first France, then Britain, controlled the country, albeit through Egyptian surrogates. Britain would maintain ownership and control of the Suez Canal until 1956.

While the Egyptian elite had become westernized, most of the country was poor and traditional. When WWI broke out, the Ottoman Empire sided with Germany, the already complicated regional politics became ever more complex. Soon after the war started, Ruth joined the Red Cross.

To protect its interests in the region, Britain formed the Arab Bureau. Its most notable member was T.H. Lawrence, popularly known as Lawrence of Arabia. Because of her vast knowledge of the region, the men of the Arab Bureau plucked Gertrude out of the Red Cross to work with them.

Though she had no formal military training or rank, Gertrude was referred to as Major Miss Bell. Politically, Gertrude Bell and T.H. Lawrence were of similar minds. They both believed that, in the long run, it was in British interests to allow for Arab and Persian independence.

During WWI, T.H. Lawrence repeatedly risked his life helping local militias attack Ottoman forces. Gertrude did not fight herself, but her political influence was on par with that of Lawrence. She wrote an influential position paper titled *Self-determination in Mesopotamia*. In 1920, after the war, a conference was held in Cairo. A photograph taken at the time depicts Gertrude Bell, T.H. Lawrence, and Winston Churchill astride camels with the pyramids dramatically seen in the background.

The agreements reached in the conference rewarded the Arabs who had fought with the British against the Ottomans. In particular, due to Bell's influence, The Turkish Province of Mesopotamia became the country of Iraq. Delegates to the conference agreed that Faisal of Arabia would become the King of Iraq. About her role in the Cairo conference, Gertrude wrote, "I'll never engage in the creating of Kings again. It is too great a strain."

After the conference, Gertrude served as an advisor to the King she helped anoint. As an advisor, she helped establish a law that kept archaeological finds in Iraq. With the King's support, contributions, and Gertrude Bell's own collection, the Baghdad Archeological Museum came into being.

Iraqis referred to Gertrude as Al-Khatun. Al-Khatun can be translated as Queen, but not necessarily a literal Queen. Calling Gertrude Al-Khatun was like saying Aretha Franklin was the Queen of Soul. In Gertrude Bell's case, being called Al-Khatun meant she typified what a good Queen should be: honest, tactful, intelligent, and supportive.

Gertrude Bell had many close but non-romantic relationships with several men, William Ramsay, T.H. Lawrence, and King Faisal, among others. She had a few romantic interests as well. Her first significant love was, in 1892, with a man named Cadogan. Cadogan was a member of the British Foreign Service. However, Cadogan was a known gambler. Her father disapproved of the relationship, and Gertrude, acting on the counsel of her father, ended the relationship.

Another love interest was Sir Frank Sweetenham, a British administrator in Singapore. Gertrude and Sweetenham met in Singapore when she visited the colony in 1903 with her brother. Gertrude and Sir Frank briefly renewed their relationship in England when he was on home leave. Gertrude and Sweethenham continued a regular correspondence until 1909. Many years later, on the grounds of her insanity, Sweethenham divorced his wife.

Around 1912, Gertrude became involved with another married man, Charles Wylie. Wylie was a major in the British army. From 1913 to 1915, the two exchanged love letters regularly. Sources say that while Gertrude and Wylie shared an attraction to each other, the relationship never became sexual. In the early 20th century, a respectable woman did not have sex outside of marriage. Gertrude was likely a lifelong virgin.

Even if the relationships were romantic but non-sexual, why did Gertrude become involved with married men? Maybe being romantically involved (even if not sexually) with married men was a "safe thing" for Gertrude. Such men would not tie her down. Without a husband, Gertrude would be free to live life as she wanted, excavating ruins, climbing mountains, and just having an adventuresome life.

Still, Gertrude's passion for Wylie was genuine. If Wylie, for some reason, had found himself a widower, and he and Gertrude married, the course might have been different and the map of the Middle (or Near) East vastly different. However, Wylie died in 1915 in the disastrous Gallipoli campaign, a campaign Churchill had vigorously supported. In 1920, as Gertrude sat on her camel next to Churchill and T.H. Lawrence, one wonders whether she thought more about how Churchill had sent Wylie to his death or the country she helped create.

On July 12, 1926, in Baghdad, two days short of her 58th birthday, Gertrude Bell died. She had taken some sleeping pills. Whether she died in an intentional suicide or an accidental overdose is unclear. Whatever the case, the oppressive heat in Baghdad in July and her health problems likely hastened her death. Despite much anti-Western sentiment in Iraq, one wing of the Iraqi national museum remains named after her.

In the 1996 movie *The English Patient*, British soldiers are seen reviewing a map before heading into a mountain pass. Trying to reassure the others, one soldier remarks, "The Bell map shows the way." The other replies, "Let's hope *he* is right." The "he," of course, was Gertrude Bell.

BEING on the THRONE (or the Power Behind)

Introduction:

Leaders need legitimacy. Legitimacy can come from a freely held election. However, throughout most of history, kingdoms, and empires were ruled by kings and emperors, not freely elected Presidents, or Prime Ministers. When a king or emperor died, the king or emperor's firstborn son, if of sufficient age, was assumed to be the legitimate new king.

The largest empire of all time was the British Empire. The British Empire was at its height in the 19th century when Queen Victoria was on the throne. She ascended the throne in 1837 only because she had no brothers or male cousins. Had there been a brother or male cousin, Victoria would have been a footnote in history.

In 2013, the United Kingdom's law of succession was changed. Upon the death of the king or queen, the firstborn, if of sufficient age, becomes the new sovereign.

In our first example, legitimacy was conferred on Boudica by her late husband Prasutagas's will. Prasutagas was the king of the Antedios, a small tribe in modern-day England. In his will, Prasutagas bequeathed half the kingdom to his wife. However, the Romans didn't consider Prasutagus a "real king."

Our second example concerns the Mongol Empire. The Mongol Empire was the second-largest empire in history. After Genghis Khan died, his third son, Ogodei, became the Great Khan. When Ogodei went off to war, his wife, Torogene, ruled in her husband's absence.

While not as large as the British or Mongol Empire, the Ottoman Empire lasted an impressive six-hundred years. Many consider Sulieman the Magnificent as the most effective sultan to rule the Ottoman Empire. For much of Sulieman's long reign, his wife Hasfa was his chief adviser.

The most influential female monarch of all time was Empress Dowager Cixi of China. Cixi was born in 1835 when the Industrial Revolution was in full swing in the West. By 1869, the US had a transcontinental railroad. Cixi supported many aspects of modernizing China but was hesitant about railroads. China did not get its first railroad until 1876.

Finally, we will consider civil rights leader Mary Bethune. Her friendship with another influential woman, Eleanor Roosevelt, helped her legitimacy, in large part. However, most of Mary Bethune's legitimacy was self-earned. Mary was the legitimate, if unofficial, leader of a group of influential African-American men and repeatedly elected, and therefore a legitimate leader of various women's groups.

Boudica

Boudica was born in A.D. 25 in what the Romans called Britannia. The people of Britannia were organized into several tribes. By convention, the leaders of these tribes have been referred to as kings, but tribal chiefs would be more accurate. In the first century, the Roman Empire was Europe's undisputed superpower. Boudica would take the fight to the most powerful army in the world.

When Boudica was twenty-one years old, the Roman emperor Caligula was assassinated by The Praetorian Guards, the elite unit specifically tasked with guarding the emperor. The Praetorian Guards, like almost everyone else, were simply fed up with Caligula's excesses. The Praetorian Guards anointed Caligula's nephew Claudius, as emperor. Claudius, though, was not considered "emperor material." He had a limp, stuttered, and lacked military experience.

In part to prove he was worthy of the title of emperor; Claudius ordered an invasion of Britannia. The disciplined, well-trained, well-armed Roman armies soon pacified much of southern Britannia. Claudius joined the fight just enough to receive a triumph, a military parade upon his return. (He would not be the only emperor to claim credit for a war his generals fought).

While Claudius was still in Britannia, eleven "kings," including Antedios, the "king" of the Iceni tribe (the tribe to which Boudica belonged), pledged their support for the new emperor. However, the "kings" may simply have thought they were pledging to ongoing peaceful relations and good trade. Many expected the Romans to leave—just as Caesar had done nearly a century before. However, Rome had other plans.

Roman legionnaires began reshaping Britannia to their liking, particularly in the town of Camulodunum. Traditionally, a legionnaire who had fought for Rome for twenty-five years often received a grant of land for retirement. Camulodunum was shaping up to be a Roman retirement community. This did not sit well with the locals. Several tribes, including the Iceni, rebelled. They attacked the Roman forces. The rebellion was ineffective, and King Antedios was one of its victims. Boudica's husband Prasutagus then became "King" of the Iceni.

Prasutagus was a vassal-king. Vassal kings often had some independence in local affairs. Allowing a local king a shred of independence was good policy. It helped keep the peace and allowed Roman armies to be dispatched elsewhere in the empire. However, sometimes raw politics trumped good empire management.

Claudius died in 54 A.D., and Nero became emperor. Nero, as was customary, had his predecessor, Claudius, declared a God—one of the many gods in the Roman pantheon. Roman officials erected a temple to Claudius in Camulodunum. As Roman subjects, the Iceni and the other tribes were expected to worship Claudius. However, the Iceni and the other tribes were Druids. They did not want to worship any Roman God, especially one who had turned their kingdom into Roman territory. Further, despite their sworn allegiance to Rome, the Iceni still considered Prasutagus their King, not Nero.

Like other vassal kings, Prasutagus walked a fine line. If he acted too Roman, he would not be considered a king. If he acted too kingly, he risked Rome's wrath. Likely thinking he was acting "like a Roman," Prasutagus made out a will. Prasutagus was likely illiterate in Latin (or any other language) and used a scribe to make out his will. A scribe that was likely a Roman. A scribe whose allegiance unquestionably belonged to Rome. A loyal scribe would have undoubtedly reported the contents of the will to his superiors.

In the will, Prasutagus bequeathed half his estate to the emperor Nero and the other half to his wife, Boudica and her sister. Prasutagus likely considered the half-and-half provisions more than fair. However, such division implied that the riches of the kingdom (mostly grain) were the Iceni's to give to Rome and were not already Rome's possessions.

Whether because of the will or another factor, Suetonius wanted the local population to understand Rome was in charge. Suetonius marched against the city of Mona, a Druid stronghold. Some of the defenders were armed women. (The defenders had ignored a previous Roman governor's edict to surrender their arms).

Initially, the legionnaires hesitated to attack the defenders as some were women, but Suetonius insisted. The defenders were no match for the disciplined and better-armed Roman army. King Prasutagus died either in the battle or shortly thereafter, and Boudica became Queen. To underscore Rome's supremacy, after the battle, Suetonius cut down a small forest that the Druids considered sacred. There would be no gods but Roman Gods. This desecration further incensed the Iceni.

After Prasutagus' death, a Roman bureaucrat named Decianus arrived at the Iceni capital to take possession of Rome's full share. A military detachment accompanied Decianus. As he and his staff cataloged what they considered belonged to Rome, Queen Boudica protested.

For her temerity to question what belonged to Rome, Decianus had Boudica flogged, and her daughters raped. Boudica's daughters would have been no older than fifteen. Historic UK's website states that the men who raped the daughters were Roman slaves. However, this is likely an embellishment. Much more likely, Decianus granted the "privilege" of raping the daughters to favored officers.

In the days and weeks that followed, Boudica plotted her revenge. She marshaled her countrymen and countrywomen to rebel. To signify her commitment, Boudica adorned herself with a metal band around her neck, an adornment normally worn only by a chieftain. She also put on a special scarf. Donning the band and scarf indicated the wearer was prepared to die rather than surrender.

Boudica gathered her forces around the Calmundum. Aware of the propaganda value it would provide, Boudica arranged for operatives inside the city to tear down the statue of Claudius before the battle. The Roman forces quickly realized they needed reinforcements. They sent word to Decianus, who had gone to Londinium (modern-day London).

Perhaps underestimating the need for reinforcements because a woman was at the head of the army, Decianus sent only two hundred soldiers. The Iceni slaughtered the small force. A second relief column of 2,500, including cavalry, was also ambushed. Boudica set Calmundum ablaze. There would be no retirement community for former Roman soldiers.

Boudica's next turned to Londinium. However, by the time she and her army arrived at Londinium, Decianus had made his way to the safety of Gaul (France). Further, before Boudica's expected attack on Londinium, Suetonius ordered his troops to abandon the city. Suetonius wanted to take on Boudica on his terms.

With no army to fight her in Londinium, Boudica exacted revenge on Roman collaborators, particularly the women. Some of the richest women in the city, those who had profited the most from collaboration with Rome, were hung. Others had their bodies desecrated and impaled on poles. Boudica exacted her revenge for the rape of her daughters on the women who had collaborated with Rome.

The residents of another town, Verulamium (modern-day St. Albans), met a similar fate. Verulamium had belonged to a tribe that had long aligned itself with Rome. In very short order, Boudica had taken three cities from Rome.

A showdown between Boudica and a Roman army was inevitable. The exact location of the battle is unknown, but it is believed that the Roman army was at least partially hidden by a forest. From their hidden positions, the Romans could see that most of Boudica's forces were women.

Before the battle, Boudica, like other generals throughout history, rode up and down her line of troops, inspiring them to fight hard. Marshaling up and down the line of troops, atop a chariot, with her hair flowing, Boudica impressed even the Roman commanders. Before the battle began, like at Mona, the Roman troops had to be assured that it was acceptable to attack armed women.

While Boudica's bravery was impressive, using the advantage of terrain, their javelins, and most importantly, their tight discipline, the Roman army slaughtered Boudica's forces. According to the Roman historian Tacitus, only 400 Roman soldiers lost their lives, while rebel losses were 80,000. The figure of 80,000 rebel losses is no doubt an exaggeration. However, if the correct number of rebel losses is one-tenth as many, that would still be a twenty-to-one kill ratio. It was more a slaughter than a battle.

Boudica was not killed in the melee. However, Like Cleopatra before her, Boudica committed suicide instead of being captured. If captured, she would have paraded in a military triumph on the streets of Rome as war booty. She would not submit herself to such indignity.

While Rome decisively won the battle, Boudica's earlier successes gave Rome pause. They sent more reinforcements. Still, the demand for local control continued. Rebels destroyed a few Roman vessels and otherwise harassed the Romans. Rome began appointing governors that ruled with a lighter touch. A *Pax Romana* prevailed and held for three centuries. While Boudica lost her final battle, her people won the war.

In 1903, a statue of Boudica was erected in London. It depicts Boudica in her chariot. While often ignored by tourists and locals alike, her statue stands by Westminster Bridge, just across the river from Parliament.

Toregene and Fatima

The story of Toregene and Fatima must begin with the life of Genghis Khan. Genghis Khan was born Temujin in 1158. Temujin's father was a minor chieftain and had multiple wives, as was common for chiefs. Temjuin was born to a second wife. Through a complex series of events that included much luck, political skill, bravery, and murder, Temujin unified the Mongol people and became Genghis Khan.

Genghis Khan conquered his enemies with much brutality. Thousands were taken as slaves. As his reputation for savagery became known, many towns surrendered to the Mongols without a fight. Being conquered by the Mongols was not necessarily a bad thing. Accepting Mongol rule meant enjoying the protection of the strongest army anywhere in Eurasia.

Unlike Mongol chieftains of the past, Genghis Khan made appointments by merit—even former enemies could be placed in positions of considerable responsibility. Genghis Khan also promoted religious tolerance. He also instituted a postal system. A postal system similar to Pony Express, but which would become ten times larger.

Genghis Khan had many wives and many concubines. He took some wives and concubines as spoils of war; others were given to him for political purposes. He had so many wives and concubines that some academics suggest that one percent of those living in Asia today are descendants of Genghis Khan.

Genghis's first wife was named Borte. When they were pre-teens, Borte and Temujin were betrothed. As a teenager, Borte was abducted by a rival tribe. (A common practice). Heroically, Temujin rescued her from captivity, and they began living together as husband and wife.

Borte bore four sons from Genghis Khan. Her third son, Ogodei, became a competent commander but wasn't the brilliant tactician or inspirational figure his father was. Ogodei was already in command of a significant portion of the Mongol Army when, as a symbol of his submission to Genghis Khan, a defeated tribal chief gave one of his wives, a woman named Toregene, to Ogodei. In the later years of his life, Genghis Khan selected Ogodei as his successor as Khan's two older sons quarreled severely.

While Genghis Kahn indicated his preference for Ogodei, in Mongol society, succession and legitimacy as a khan did not necessarily pass from father to son. According to tradition, there was a two-year waiting period before tribal leaders would gather to pick a new chief. Often, but not always, the new chief was the first-born son of the previous khan. The two-year waiting interlude had two purposes: One was simple respect for the recently deceased chief. The other was to allow for "politicking" so that the new khan would be elected by acclamation and tribal harmony preserved.

Genghis Khan died on August 18, 1227. After the customary two-year waiting period, Ogodei was elected Great Khan. He established Karakorum as the first Mongol capital. Frequently relying on the sage advice of his generals, Ogodei continued to expand the Mongol empire. When Ogodci was off making war, his wife Toregene ruled in the new capital. (Ogodei's first wife, Boraqchin, had no sons, so Toregene became the de facto first wife).

Under Torogene's administration, Karakorum became a functioning capital, with a civil administration. There was also funding for schools and other construction. When Ogodei was off making war and visiting dignitaries arrived in the capital, the dignitaries did business with Torogene. Among the dignitaries Toregene received were: the Seljuk Sultan, competing claimants to the Georgia throne, a Russian prince, and envoys from the Caliph, the supreme leader of Sunni Muslims.

Toregene's closest confidant was a woman named Fatima. Fatima, like Toregene, was taken as war booty some years before. Almost certainly, Toregene and Fatima became lovers.

When he periodically returned home from war, one wonders what Ogodei thought. Was he pleased to see his wife ably administering government in his absence? Or was he envious of her administrative skills? What did he think of his wife's close relationship with Fatima? Did he feel inadequate? Marginalized? As Khan, Ogodei could do as he pleased. He easily could have dismissed his wife and appointed any of his generals to govern in his absence, but he didn't. He saw his wife doing a good job administering the country, perhaps even better than he could do himself. As for feelings toward Fatima, who knows?

Like many Mongol men (and women), Ogodei drank heavily. In the last few years, his drinking became particularly excessive. Most scholars agree that

Ogodei's excessive drinking led to his death on December 11, 1241, in present-day Hungary. Your author speculates that three factors drove the excessive drinking: Ogodei didn't measure up to his father as a general, his wife proved to be a more capable administrator than he would have been, and he was jealous of his wife's intimacy with Fatima.

After her husband's death, Toregene's power grew. She dismissed most of her late husband's advisers and appointed women to governorships. She also formally elevated Fatima to the chief counselor and continued with a taxation plan. (Under Genghis Khan, most income came from booty gained through military action).

Toregene's power was such that she delayed the conclave to elect a new Great Khan for an additional three years past the traditional two years interim. Using her considerable political capital, Toregene positioned her son, Guyuk, to be elected as Great Khan. It was a decision she would regret.

Toregene had another son, Koden. For reasons which are not clear, Koden claimed that his mother's chief counselor, Fatima, was a witch. Female shamans were accepted as part of Mongol culture; the accusation that Fatima was a witch was likely merely a pretext. Pretext or not, Guyuk listened to what Koden said about Fatima and ordered Fatima seized. Toregene protested vehemently.

Guyuk ignored his mother's pleas and had Fatima executed. To lead credibility to the "witch theory," Guyuk ordered Fatima's bodily orifices to be shut (to avoid evil spirits escaping). He had Fatima's body thrown into a river to suppress further any evil spirits. Toregene never forgave her son for murdering Fatima. She died a year and a half later of unknown causes.

As of 2021, Mongolia had four female cabinet ministers and several female ambassadors. While bordered by Russia and China, ethnically Mongolians are most closely related to the citizens of most Stan countries, i.e. (Kazakhstan, Kyrgyzstan, etc.). In Kazakhstan, International Women's Day is a state holiday, and its Parliament passed Kazakhstan's equivalent of the Equal Rights Amendment. Further, when Kyrgyzstan was still part of the Soviet Union, its president was a woman. (She later became Kyrgyzstan's first ambassador to the United States). The influence of Toregene, and the other Mongolian women who ruled as regents, has a long shadow.

Hurrem Sultcan (aka Roxelana)

Hurrem Sultan, aka Roxelana, was born in 1502 in what is now modern-day Ukraine. Her father was a Russian Orthodox priest. Russian Orthodox priests may marry. Her birth name is lost to history, but in the West, we know her as Roxelana. Some sources say her invented European name, Roxelana, was inspired by her red hair. Others say it is a reference to her native language of Ruthenian. Ruthenian being to modern Ukrainian what Middle English is to modern English. In her late teens, the Tartars captured Roxelana. At age twenty, her future mother-in-law Hafsa Sultan purchased her as a slave.

When Hafsa's son, Suleiman, became sultan, Hafsa became the Valide Sultan, or, to use Anglicized terminology, the queen mother. Likely as a coronation present, Hafsa gifted Roxelana to her son. The gifting of slaves was a common practice in the Ottoman Empire. Why Hafsa gifted Roxelana, in particular, is unclear. Perhaps, so that her son might gain insights into Empire's Christian rivals, Hafsa wanted her son to have a European concubine. Or maybe gifting a slave to him was no more than a whim. Whatever Hafsa's motivation, she had the means to buy and gift a slave independently.

In the West, because of his skill as a general, and because he often, but not always, showed mercy to his enemies, Suleiman became known as Suleiman the Magnificent. Like other sultans, Sulieman wore two hats. As sultan, he was the secular leader of the Ottoman Empire. As Caliph, he was the "Pope" for Sunni Muslims. During his long rule, Suleiman standardized judicial practice. His legal code continued well after his death. His legal decrees included protections for Jews. In the Muslim world, his title is Suleiman, the Lawgiver.

The capital of the Ottoman Empire was Istanbul, a major center of commerce. In the harem, Roxelana undoubtedly ate a much more varied diet than she would have in Ukraine. In the harem, servants prepared food. Had she remained the daughter of a priest, she would have helped her mother cook. Once she married, undoubtedly, she would have cooked for her husband. Also, as a child, Roxelana no doubt was familiar with the smell of farm animals. In the harem, Roxelana enjoyed the smell of perfume. Another major change would have involved the climate. In winter, Istanbul is a lot warmer than her native Ukraine.

However, life in the gilded cage of the harem often came at a heavy price. Eunuchs guarded women in the harem and women didn't leave the palace often. Even more seriously, when a concubine had a son, when the son reached adulthood, he could be slain. Killing the son prevented a power struggle between half-brothers when the sultan died. More fortunate sons were sent off to administer some remote part of the empire, and their mothers often went with them.

Harems have a pecking order. The sultan's favorite concubine sat at the top, and older concubines, those past their child-bearing years, were at the very bottom. Before Roxelana, Suleiman's favorite concubine was Mahidevran. Mahidevran had already provided Suleiman with a male heir, her son Mustafa. However, Suleiman soon picked Roxelana over Mahidevran. Why Roxelana became Suleiman 's favorite is not clear. It might have been because of her hair. As a European woman, especially a woman with red hair, she was not like the others in the harem. Her beauty was unique. Roxelana was, unlike most of the women in the harem, literate. Suleiman may have found her intellect attractive. Or, as his mother may have intended, Suleiman's initial attraction to Roxelana may have been what he could learn about his Christian rivals.

It is plausible that a combination of her beauty, intellect, and knowledge of her native land and other Christian places is what drew Suleiman to her. Whatever Suleiman's initial attraction to Roxelana and hers to him, a genuine relationship developed. Over time, Roxelana learned to speak and write Turkish and converted to Islam. Her conversion appears to be genuine. Had Roxelana remained a Christian, she would not have reached the top of the pecking order.

Roxelana and Suleiman married around 1524, and she became Hurren Sultana. During their marriage, Roxelana and Suleiman had five boys and one girl. So, in terms of succession, there was an heir and four spares. When Suleiman and Roxelana married, Mustafa lost his status as the heir apparent. Suleiman sent Mustafa to govern a rural province. His mother went with him.

Suleiman reigned the Ottoman Empire for forty-six years, the longest reign in the six-hundred-year history of the empire. When Suleiman met with foreign dignitaries in court, Hurren literally hid behind the throne, discreetly offering her counsel. Moreover, Suleiman undoubtedly used Hurren as a sounding board in his standardization of the legal code. Suleiman recognized his wife's worth and paid her a substantial salary. She was one of the highest-paid members of the royal court.

Like Ogodei, Sulieman was often away from the capital making war. In her husband's absence, Hurren corresponded with the King of Poland, the only woman in the Ottoman Empire to have had directly and officially written another head of state. While Suleiman was away, Hurren provided her husband with updates about the goings-on in the capital. Her letters, and his to her, were also personal. She sometimes used poetry to express her love. Hurren Sultana must have been a very intelligent woman. Learning to speak a second language in adulthood is challenging enough. Being able to write, especially poetry, using a different alphabet is exceptionally impressive.

During Suleiman's rule, a fire destroyed much of the palace that housed the harem. Hurren had the harem quarters rebuilt closer to the royal court. Moving the harem closer to the court was an indication not only of Hurren's independent authority but also showed how secure she was in her relationship with her husband. (After all, how many women would want a harem next door to their husband's office?)

On her own authority, but no doubt with her husband's knowledge and encouragement, Hurren established a mosque, two schools, and what, in today's terminology, would be called a soup kitchen.

As in other empires, there was much palace intrigue in the Ottoman Empire. Suleiman, likely without cause, suspected that Mustafa, his firstborn son, wanted to seize the throne. Suleiman ordered Mustafa executed. How much Hurren had a role in getting her husband to execute his firstborn son is subject to debate. Whatever role she played, she didn't act alone. Suleiman's grand vizier also supported the execution. The empire needed a clear line of succession, and executing Mustafa kept that line unaltered. Without her son's income, Mahidevran fell into poverty.

Hurren died in 1558. She did not live to see her son ascend the throne. Shortly after a pyrrhic victory in modern-day Hungary, Suleiman died. His heart was buried near the battle. To assure political stability, his death was hidden for six weeks. His body (less the heart) was returned to the capital for burial. Hurren's son, Selim, then assumed the throne.

Despite Islamic prohibition against alcohol, Selim drank heavily and proved to be a weak leader. During his reign and the reigns of subsequent leaders equally uninspired, women wielded the power behind the throne. Historians refer to this period as the Sultanate of Women.

Selim is credited with doing one thing of importance. He bought a house for Mahidevran, the mother of his slain half-brother, and otherwise allowed her to live out her days in modest comfort.

Turkey allowed women to vote in 1930 well before Italy or Switzerland. In 1993, Turkey had a female prime minister. In 2011, Turkey was the first of 35 countries to sign an accord, the Turkey Convention, which called for gender equality and the protection of women. However, in July 2021, Turkey withdrew from the accord which bears its name.

Cixi, The Empress Dowager

While she is well-known in Asia, few in the West know about the life of Cixi, the Empress Dowager. Cixi's father was a very minor noble and a mid-level bureaucrat. In Imperial China, nobles, scholars, and most bureaucrats were literate. However, the vast majority of the population was illiterate. There was no public education system. Children learned from tutors. Cixi may have learned to read from her father, he may have hired tutors, or perhaps she had a combination of the two. Also, in a highly unusual situation for the times, Cixi and her father often discussed politics.

Cixi's family was of Manchu, not Han, ancestry. For many generations, the upper echelon of the imperial bureaucracy, like the emperor, had been Manchu, not Han. As a Manchu, Cixi did not have to have bound feet like Han girls born into relative wealth. Having bound feet was a status symbol and implied one had servants. Lower-class Han girls, of which there were millions, had unbound feet, feet that helped till the family farm.

In 1850, the emperor died, and his nineteen-year-old son succeeded him. As per custom, the newly installed emperor was entitled to add concubines to the harem. Cixi, like many other young women, each in their own sedan chair, was taken to the place by court officials to be considered as a concubine. Cixi made the cut. Most of the other young women did not. Some were married off to or became concubines for lesser nobles. Those not chosen were returned to their families.

The Chinese harem had a formal pecking order. There were nine ranks of concubines. Cixi, as a novice entrant, was accorded the sixth rank. As in the harem of the Ottoman Empire, the Chinese Imperial harem used eunuchs as guards. There were also many servants. Even as a sixth-rank concubine, Cixi had multiple servants. She and her servants were given a generous food allotment. Famine was a common occurrence in China and a common cause of rebellion.

Eunuchs and servants could be beaten at will. Yet, they were usually steadfast in their loyalty. Having an "iron rice bowl" had its benefits.

Accustomed to talking with her father about political matters, as the emperor discussed a revolt in an outlying province, Cixi offered her opinion. However, for a concubine to tell the emperor how to handle a revolt was hugely offensive. The emperor could have ordered Cixi executed. Fortunately for Cixi, the emperor's wife, Empress Zhen, interceded, and Cixi received a harsh admonishment instead.

Over time, Cixi became a concubine of the fifth rank. Then, after six years in the harem, Cixi gave birth to a boy. Having a boy elevated Cixi to being number two consort, right behind Empress Zhen. On August 22, 1861, young Emperor Xianfeng died, and Cixi's five-year-old son became emperor.

In western monarchies, when a child emperor ascends to the throne, one person is usually appointed to act as regent. In Imperial China, a Board of Regents rules in a young emperor's name. The regents for Cixi's son were vehemently anti-western and considered Chinese culture superior to all other cultures. Western Imperialism is full of examples where western values and Christianity were believed to be superior to the religion and culture of "the lesser races." However, such arrogance also went the other way.

The imperial court of China was exceedingly ceremonial. Having an audience with the emperor meant having to prostrate or "kowtow" before any discussion could begin. The refusal of western officials to kowtow was a great affront to most Chinese. Also, royal decrees had to have the proper stamps. Cixi and Zhen used imperial stamps on artwork. Cixi and Zhen reminded the board that it was proper protocol for their highnesses to stamp decrees issued in the emperor's name. The Board of Regents expected their highnesses to "rubber stamp" any decrees.

The anti-western Board of Regents ordered thirty-nine western diplomats arrested. Some of those taken prisoner were tortured in the classic Chinese method of "death by a thousand cuts." As part of a rescue mission and in retaliation for the diplomats' abduction, the French and the British burned and looted much of the summer palace complex. The Board of Regents wanted revenge.

Cixi, like the late emperor's half-brother, Prince Chun, and another royal, Prince Gong, feared provoking the West would only lead to more retaliation. These two men saw that Cixi could lead China on a better path. Knowing she had the support of Chun and Gong, Cixi issued and stamped her own decrees. She directed two of the board members to commit suicide. Which they did. A particularly corrupt official was subjected to death by a thousand cuts. The other regents found themselves dismissed. Cixi's coup was successful. She was just twenty-six years old. Her son, the emperor, was five.

Prince Gong was appointed to lead the newly established Grand Council that would rule in the emperor's name. Cixi and Prince Gong would have a nearly lifelong, platonic relationship. As Prince Gong held court, Cixi and Empress Zhen sat behind a partition, literally, they were the power behind the throne.

Behind the scenes, Empress Zhen focused on royal appointments. Of which there were hundreds. Cixi handled policy. With Cixi and Zhen in charge, Chinese relations with the West took a dramatic turn for the better. They continued to improve after Zhen's death. A British national, Thomas Wade, developed a system to render the Chinese language in the Roman (A to Z) alphabet. Another Brit, Robert Hart, was put in charge of the collection of customs duties. An American, Frederick Ward, trained thousands of Chinese soldiers and helped suppress a serious rebellion. Another American, Anson Burlingame, on behalf of Cixi, negotiated a "treaty of equality" between the United States and China. These men served Cixi well. Western officials, unlike many Chinese officials, were known for being incorruptible.

Cixi did not accept all the West had to offer. She resisted installing telegraph lines and employing modern mining techniques, but most of all, she resisted the construction of rail lines. Her opposition was partly cultural and partly environmental. Proposed rail lines could disturb ancestral burial plots and otherwise run counter to the Chinese notion of Feng Shui. Further, Cixi didn't want the dirty exhaust from locomotives to foul the air.

Even though she was running China, Cixi still lived in the harem and eunuchs attended her. Little An was Cixi's favorite eunuch. Cixi enjoyed his company and, apparently to the extent he was able, provided her physical pleasure as well as companionship.

Cixi sent Little An on an errand to buy clothes for her son's upcoming royal wedding. Normally, eunuchs were not allowed to leave the palace, but Cixi wanted to give her favorite eunuch a break.

Despite authorization from Cixi, a local governor arrested Little An and sought to have him executed. The royal court, including the modern-thinking Prince Gong, agreed with the governor. Little An was beheaded, as were several other eunuchs and bodyguards who had accompanied him. Empress Cixi was distraught for weeks. One official who had pressed the hardest for Little An's execution was the emperor's uncle, Prince Zhun. Cixi waited for the right moment to seek her revenge.

In 1875, Cixi's son, the emperor, died. After her son's death, Empress Cixi and Empress Zhen issued a decree that, honoring the late emperor's wishes, the two of them would designate a new emperor. They decreed they would adopt Prince Zhun's young son. Prince Zhun was furious. As per tradition, Zhun's son would be taken from his care and raised in the palace. Cixi had exacted her revenge.

Cixi adopted two slogans: Make China Strong, and Make Chinese Rich. Under these slogans, and through Prince Gong and another man, Earl Li, the government sent several emissaries abroad. They returned with modern mining technology and the principles of private enterprise, including the sale of shares of stock. However, Cixi still hesitated about building a rail system. China did not lay the first track until 1889.

Western powers still tried to bully China. France insisted China withdraw its forces from Vietnam and demanded payment of an indemnity. Not wishing to provoke a war, China agreed to withdraw its forces but balked at paying an indemnity. After a battle in which the French were defeated, France capitulated. France accepted Vietnam without paying an indemnity. Cixi also concluded treaties with Russia and Britain.

In 1881, Cixi's best friend, Empress Zhen, died. Three years later, she had to force her go-to advisor, Prince Gong, to resign. With her favorite advisor sent out to pasture, her closest friend deceased, and with the only love of her life, Little An, beheaded, Cixi was lonely.

In 1889, Cixi's seventeen-year-old adopted son assumed the throne, and Cixi no longer ruled as regent. Her influence in setting policy was nil. In a "if life gives you lemons, make lemonade" situation, Cixi made the most of her political exile. She bred dogs, took up painting, and sponsored and revised Chinese opera. She also developed friendships with a few Western women.

Despite Cixi's modernization, China's military was still inferior. Japan pressed this advantage. In a series of lopsided battles, Japan seized significant territory. After seizing a major port, Japan offered peace. The terms were steep. Japan wanted 230 million Taels as an indemnity. China had just paid off to western powers 41 million Taels. Payment of such a huge indemnity meant raising taxes *and* diverting all of China's customs duties to Japan.

Despite battlefield losses, hundreds of officials wanted to fight for more favorable terms, and Cixi agreed. Still, the young emperor agreed to peace on Japan's terms. His popularity, which was already modest, plummeted. The western powers further exploited China's weakness. They signed treaties with France, Germany, and Britain. Treaties that allowed the western powers "to lease" parts of China. Britain's control of Hong Kong would last until January 1, 1997.

The young emperor eventually realized he was in over his head and brought his adoptive mother out of exile. Cixi and Guangxu pledged to work for a better China. To emphasize that China was modernizing and together they were working to make a better China, Cixi and Guangxu, in a publicity stunt, rode one of China's first trains together. Also, as part of modernization, more envoys went abroad.

Upon returning to China, breaking his pledge to work with his adoptive mother, Guangzu met privately with a former envoy named Youwei Kang. Kang flattered the young emperor and persuaded him to sack many officials. When she learned of her adoptive son's betrayal, Cixi was outraged.

Kang wanted to be the power behind the throne for himself. He wanted a former Japanese prime minister, Hirbumi Ito, to serve as Prime Minster. Through Ito, Kang would control Emperor Guangzu. To succeed in his plot, Kang also needed the Chinese military, weak as it was, to be on his side and sought the support of a general named Yuan.

Yuan, however, was loyal to the monarchy. Yuan revealed Kang's machinations during a royal audience. He did not directly implicate the emperor, but it was common knowledge that Guangzu and Kang were close. After the royal audiences finished for the day, Cixi had her son placed under house arrest. From then on, Cixi was in charge, and her adoptive son became a figurehead. Guangxu did not seriously protest being marginalized. Further, despite his youth, Guangzu suffered from an incurable kidney disorder. He accepted Cixi's suggestion to adopt a child so the dynasty could continue. He adopted a fourteen-year-old boy. Even with formidable Cixi on the throne, Western powers wanted China to run their way. Italy demanded a port concession. German troops burned down several houses because of anti-Christian rioting, rioting that was triggered by missionaries turning a Chinese temple into a church.

Much of the initial unrest was in Shandon. Shandon was a city known for a unique form of martial arts similar to boxing. Hence, those revolting against the west and the monarchy became known as Boxers. The Boxer's Rebellion was a grass-roots effort to push out the western powers. The western powers wanted the "Boxers" quashed and took things into their hands. To suppress the Boxers, the western powers stationed twenty-thousand well-armed and well-trained troops on Chinese soil. The Boxers, who were far more numerous, put up considerable resistance but were ill-equipped and had more bravery than training.

Foreign troops increasingly gained the upper hand. Many Chinese feared the monarchy would fall and tried to curry favor with the foreigners. Cixi, without trial, had several officials executed. Troops were marching toward the capital, and it was clear the capital would fall soon. Cixi fled with a small entourage, not in a sedan chair but upon a mule. She set up a government-in-exile in a provincial capital, over six hundred miles away. With foreign troops in the capital, Cixi had a weak hand. Yet, provincial governors, all of whom were men, rallied behind her. No one wanted China ruled by foreign powers, and Cixi was the only one with legitimate power to rule all of China.

With the Boxer rebellion suppressed, the western powers were willing to give the capital back to China. However, they demanded compensation for doing what they believed China should have done itself. They agreed to an indemnity of three-hundred-forty-one million dollars. Russia and Germany got the lion's share. With the stipulation that the money, be used for public education, the United States waived its share.

Cixi returned to the palace and governed. She lifted the ban on Han-Manchu marriage. She made foot-binding illegal. She prohibited torture, including the long-practiced means of death by a thousand cuts. A free press was allowed to flourish. She made preparations for a constitutional monarchy. A treaty with Britain to gradually diminish the export of opium was concluded. Eunuchs still served at the palace but could leave the palace during off-hours and enjoy public life.

In September 1908, there was a critical meeting between Cixi and the Dalai Lama. In this meeting, Cixi assured the Dalai Lama that China would maintain a hands-off policy and allow the Tibetans to govern themselves. Decades later, to affirm that Tibet was part of China, communist officials encouraged migration to Tibet. There are now more ethnic Han Chinese in Tibet than Tibetans.

Of more immediate concern than the status of Tibet was the younger emperor's continuing close ties to Kang and his Japanese supporters. Further, Cixi was seventy-three years old and her health was declining. She knew she didn't have much longer to rule. Her overriding concern was that she did not want China to become Japan's puppet. Fearing her adoptive grandson would allow that to happen, she had him poisoned. Soon thereafter, on the last day of her life, Cixi proclaimed his widow Longyu as Empress Dowager with Cixi's two-year-old grandnephew to be the emperor with his father, Zaifeng, as regent.

Cixi had risen from a sixth-rank concubine to rule China, directly or indirectly, for nearly fifty years. Unlike Boudica, Toregene, or Fatima, whose authority began with their husbands, Cixi never married. During her long rule, she never had a satisfying and physically intimate relationship except, perhaps, with a eunuch. She had a long-standing friendship with Empress Zheng and, to a lesser extent, a few western women. Many men were fiercely loyal to Empress Cixi. Some of this loyalty was to the monarchy, but much was personal. Empress Cixi saw a better future for China. Men in authority helped her modernize China and take its rightful place among nations.

On December 9, 1911, Ziafeng resigned as regent. On Feb 12, 1912, Longyu abdicated and declared China a republic. The republic did not last long. After he consolidated his power, Chiang Kai-Shek and his nationalist party asserted a one-party rule. Corruption, however, was rampant. By 1949, the one-party rule of the nationalists got replaced by Mao Zedong and the one-party rule of the communists.

Several women were prominent in the communist revolution, and in the following decades, several women served on the politburo. However, in 2023, there was not a single woman serving on the politburo.

Mary Bethune

Prior to Franklin Roosevelt's being elected president in 1932, only a very few African-Americans had been appointed to managerial or professional positions in the federal government. After Roosevelt's election, that small amount increased to a tiny fraction. Mary Bethune was one of the very few African-American women in that tiny fraction.

Mary was born in 1875 in South Carolina. She was the fifteenth of seventeen children. Her parents had been slaves. After the Civil War, like many other former slaves, Mary's parents and their children, including Mary, worked on their former owners' plantations. At age nine, Mary could pick 250 pounds of cotton in a day.

Mary attended primary school in a one-room schoolhouse. After her local education, she first attended Scotia Seminary and then went to what is now called the Moody Bible Institute. She had hoped to become a missionary. However, missionaries need sponsors, and she could not find one. Moreover, when she graduated college, only about sixty percent of African-Americans were literate. Her talents as a teacher were needed at home.

In 1898 Mary married Albertus Bethune. They settled in South Carolina before moving to Florida. The marriage produced one son, Albert. While the couple still lived in South Carolina, Mary came under the tutelage of Lucy Laney. Laney operated a small school in the area. Even for its day, Laney's school was quite strict. Besides providing basic education, Laney's school emphasized the importance of Christian values.

In 1904, after moving to Florida, Mary opened a small school for African-American girls, and her son attended as well. Every school day started with Bible study. The girls (and presumably Albert) learned vocational skills such as dressmaking and cooking, but also math, foreign languages, and other college-prep courses. School did not end until nine p.m.

Mary's husband may have had mixed feelings about his son being in an otherwise all-girl school. His son was getting an education superior to what he would otherwise get. However, Albertus, probably like most men, had misgivings about his son learning how to cook and sew like girls. In 1908,

Albertus left Mary, but he and Mary never divorced. Ten years into the separation, Albertus died. Mary never remarried.

Mary's school struggled financially. To earn income for the school, students sold sweet potato pies, ice cream, and fish. However, a school cannot survive financially by "bake sales" alone. Mary invited prominent white men to serve on the board of trustees. She received donations from John Rockefeller and James Gamble, of Proctor and Gamble fame. Without the support of white men like Rockefeller and Gamble, Mary's school would have gone bankrupt.

Medical care in the south in the early 20th century was heavily segregated. The only hospital in the area was for whites only. When one of Mary's students came down with appendicitis. She was taken to a hospital, but staff did not admit her. She received medical attention on the hospital's porch. The indignity the student suffered spurred Mary to establish a hospital for Blacks. The hospital was completed in time to receive patients during the 1918 flu pandemic.

In 1917, the local chapter of the NACW (National Association of Colored Women) elected Mary as its president. She became president of the national organization two years later. Election to such an office legitimized her as a leader in the fight for African-American equality. Through her efforts, the NACW established an office in Washington, D.C. The NACW was the first Black-controlled organization to have an office in the nation's capital.

From 1920 to 1925, Mary also served as president of the Southeastern Federation of Colored Women's Clubs. Mary's election as president of the Southeastern Federation coincided with women getting the right to vote.

In the 1920s, politicians in the northern states began courting the Black vote. Voter suppression was still very heavily practiced in the south. African-Americans tended to vote Republican, the party of Lincoln. Republican President Calvin Coolidge invited Mary to attend a conference on child welfare. Later, Herbert Hoover, another Republican, invited Mary to a conference on children's health. It was tokenism, but at least an African-American woman had taken a step inside the door. For many, even Hoover and Coolidge's tokenism was a step too far.

In 1928, at a conference of women's clubs, Mary was the sole African-American woman to attend. Also in attendance were Eleanor

Roosevelt and her mother-in-law, Sara Roosevelt. The Roosevelt women saw how the other attendees snubbed Mary because she was Black and invited Mary to sit with them. It was the beginning of a lifelong friendship.

The stock market crash in 1929 was the beginning of the Great Depression. In 1932, Franklin Roosevelt, a Democrat, easily won the presidency. To deal with the economic depression, Roosevelt promulgated several programs collectively known as the New Deal. Still, things got worse before they got better. In 1934, the national unemployment rate was 23.6 percent, with Black unemployment estimated to be at least double the national figure. Blacks, especially in the south, didn't get their fair share of the New Deal. Still, some help trickled through. This was the first meaningful assistance for Blacks since Reconstruction. Blacks began leaving the party of Lincoln for the Democratic Party.

In 1935, Mary founded the NCNW (National Council for Negro Women). The NCNW was an umbrella organization for twenty-eight different organizations for Black women. Like whites-only women's clubs, Black women's clubs, to varying degrees, were social clubs, networking organizations, and advocacy groups.

In 1936, Mary's prominence in the NCNW led her to take an appointment as an assistant in the NYA (National Youth Administration), one of the many programs of the New Deal. The NYA, unlike the well-known CCC (Civilian Conservation Corps), provided vocational opportunities for women and men. In 1938, Mary received a promotion to Director for Negro Affairs of the NYA.

African-Americans serving in managerial or professional roles in the Roosevelt administration organized themselves into the Federation Council of Negro Affairs, or what became better known as the Black Cabinet. These men were the intelligentsia of the Black community; many worked in positions of responsibility in the Federal government, and others were lawyers, professors, or journalists writing for "Negro newspapers." Mary was not part of the intelligentsia elite. She had graduated from a very second-rate college and was likely the only member of the "Black Cabinet" that had picked cotton as a child. Yet, the men accepted her as their undisputed leader.

Within the Roosevelt administration were many southerners who were unabashed segregationists. In large ways and small, they tried to keep the influence of the Black Cabinet, and Mary, in particular, in check. One telling example is a phone call between Mary and Roosevelt's press secretary, Stephen Early. In the phone call, Early addressed Mary by her first name. In the mores of the time, using the honorific title of "Miss," "Missus," or "Mister" was expected. A white man referring to a Black man by his first name wasn't much better than calling him "Boy." Mary wanted the dignity of being a "Mrs." She told Mr. Early that if they knew each other better, she would call him by his first name. It was a powerful but diplomatic way to say, "You will treat me with respect."

Because of her profile as the leader of the "Black Cabinet," Roosevelt needed to meet with Mary. Meeting with her would help democrats get "the negro vote." Still, to accommodate the segregationists, Roosevelt did not accord Mary the honor of meeting with her in the Oval Office but met with her in a private office. Roosevelt listened attentively but made no substantive promises.

One of the major goals for Mary and the Black Cabinet was to have the military integrated. Roosevelt's staff adamantly opposed integrating the military. Their stance only hardened further with the start of WWII. However, with pressure from the Black Cabinet, there was an expansion of officer training for Blacks, albeit these officers would command only segregated units. The idea of a Black officer giving orders to white enlisted men was something that the segregationists in Roosevelt's administration would not accept, to say nothing of a Black female officer giving commands to a white man.

While the Black Cabinet could not get the military to accept integration, there were some victories. Black colleges were allowed to participate in a civilian aviation training program. Black women, like white women, could become officers in the military, albeit in non-combat roles.

The Black Cabinet also successfully repealed a civil service rule that required that photographs be submitted with job applications. Such a requirement made discrimination easier for those reviewing the applications. The Black Cabinet influenced regulations that barred discrimination in NYA and several other government programs. However, those regulations rarely included any provision to enforce the "no discrimination" rule. Also, a few agencies began applying statistical data to determine if discrimination was occurring. Such data collection was the forerunner of Affirmative Action programs.

In 1939, Congress passed the Hatch Act. On the surface, The Hatch Act just seems to be a bit of common sense rule-making. As it does today, the Hatch

Act bars government employees from using their government posts for partisan purposes. However, the impetus for the Hatch Act was the growing influence of the Black Cabinet. With the passage of the Hatch Act, Mary, as a federal employee, could not publicly advocate for policy change.

Mary's ability to influence "within the system" was further curtailed by the elimination of the NYA in 1943. Roosevelt's death in April 1945 denied her further access to the White House. With her access to the White House closed and her health worsening, Mary's political influence declined substantially.

Mary died in 1955. She lived long enough to see President Truman order the military desegregated and to meet with Martin Luther King, Jr.

The first president of the NAACP was a white woman. In 1983, Margret Wilson became the first African American woman to lead the organization, but her dismissal of a well-liked and well-admired man led to her removal. In 2022, Seanelle Hawkins was the first woman elected to the National Urban League.

ENTREPRENEURS

53

Introduction:

In this chapter on entrepreneurs, supportive men are harder to find. In yesteryear, in the pre-internet era, business was much more personal. Year after year, the farmer bought supplies from the same farm supply company. Year after year, the small business owner bought supplies from the same stationery store. Year after year, at tax time, the business owner met with the same accountant. Friendships formed. It was men doing business with men.

Mixed-gender business relationships can complicate things. Business relationships are often cemented over lunch or dinner. A businessman having a meal with another man differs from a businessman and a businesswoman enjoying a meal together. Rotary, the business organization of Middle America, typically holds monthly luncheons for its members; Rotary didn't admit women in 1989. However, resistance can work the other way, too. In 1994, when women began serving abroad on naval combat vessels, some of the greatest concerns came from the wives of sailors.

A financially successful woman changes the family dynamics. In yesteryear, it was common for male doctors to marry female nurses. In the 21st century, more women are becoming doctors than men. However, a male nurse marrying a female doctor is still extremely rare. In general, a financially successful woman, whether she is an entrepreneur, a doctor, or other professional, will probably want a man of similar status.

The economic realities of the 21st century have changed other relationships as well. In yesteryear, when men wanted to get their hair cut, they went to a male barber, and women went to female hairdressers. Nowadays, many women, and most men, get their hut cut at a unisex salon like *Supercuts* or *Fantastic Sams*. The traditional barbershop where a man got his hair cut by a man is nearly extinct. The hair salon of all-female staff with female-only customers is rare. Given the unique role hairdressers played in yesteryear, it is only proper to profile Martha Harper. Martha developed her hairdressing business into the first franchise system.

However, for our first profile, we consider Elisa Pinckney. Elisa did not have many options for a mate. She married a man dismissive of her entrepreneurial spirit. However, as a widow, Elisa dramatically changed the economics of pre-revolutionary South Carolina.

We will then consider Mary Gotthard. As a revolutionary-era businesswoman, Mary has a very unique claim to history. Mary never married, and her brother, her closest male relative, was worse than unsupportive.

In pre-revolutionary France, Marie Grosholtz had a supportive man. Her mentor, Dr. Phillipe Curtius, was the closest thing Marie had to a father figure. When he died, Marie inherited his business. Two centuries later, that small business sold for over a billion dollars.

In the last half of the 19th century and early 20th century, women-only colleges were established, and a handful of women attended previously all-male colleges. After graduation, most women became teachers or nurses, occupations still predominately female. Men continued to outnumber women in college well into the latter half 20th century.

While in yesteryear, men greatly outnumbered women in college, the vast majority of men of yesteryear did not attend college. Most men would list their occupation as farmer, blacksmith, miner, or other jobs requiring strenuous physical labor. Only a few jobs, such as barber, stork clerk, telegraph operator, or secretary, did not require strenuous physical labor or a college degree.

However, jobs like barber, stork clerk, etc., paid modestly. To make "real money," a man without a college degree could go into business. Then, as now, it takes money, aka capital, to make money. In the late 19th century, men with little access to capital and even fewer moral scruples became snake oil salesmen.

In yesteryear, women, particularly women of color, found it extremely difficult to secure the capital needed to start a business. A Black woman, if she didn't work in the fields, worked as a maid or other low-paying job. One exception was Marie Leavue. Marie, like her white, male snake oil counterparts, was a charlatan. Before her husband's death, like many women of the era, she sold handicrafts. It was only after her husband's death that Marie became a full-time and successful charlatan.

Elisa Lucas Pinckney

Elisa was born in Antigua in 1721. Her father was the lieutenant governor of the island. At age sixteen, while her father remained in Antigua, Elisa, her two younger siblings, and their mother left Antigua for South Carolina, where Elisa's father had a plantation. Soon after arriving in South Carolina, Elisa's mother died. This left Elisa head of the household and in charge of the plantation, including the plantation's slaves. She was not yet eighteen years old.

Eliza's plantation, like other plantations in the area, grew rice, not tobacco or cotton. As a landowner and slave owner, Elisa literally had access to seed money. However, even with slave labor, the plantation was only modestly profitable. Elisa wanted a better income.

To diversify her income stream, Elisa had a fig orchard planted. She could easily dry and export figs. She also planted oak trees, anticipating the use of the wood for shipbuilding. Beyond all that diversification, Elisa considered raising indigo. For use as a dye, indigo was highly prized. There was just one problem; no one had figured out how to grow indigo in South Carolina. Elisa began experimenting.

An older family friend, Charles Pinckney, learned of Elisa's plans to try growing indigo. Being genuinely concerned for her welfare, Pickney did not want Elisa to waste her time and money. He directed a messenger to tell Elisa to "come to town and partake of some of the amusements suitable to her time of life." Elisa told the messenger, "What he (Charles) may now think whims and projects may turn out well."

Elisa had already sent a test sample of indigo to England. Her father, who remained in Antigua, likely wrote a letter of introduction on her behalf. While her father supported developing indigo into a cash crop, he wanted Elisa to return to Antigua. She was twenty-two, an age when many, if not most women, had married.

Despite his dismissiveness of her plan to turn indigo into a cash crop, Elisa married Charles, forty-five and recently widowed. She was twenty-two. South Carolina was still rural then. Plantations were far apart. Elisa didn't have many other options besides Charles for a husband.

Elisa and Charles had three children. One died in infancy. Charles had no children from his first wife. When Elisa was thirty-one, Charles died of malaria. Once again, Elisa found herself the head of the household. Her responsibilities included not only her own children, but her younger siblings, her family's plantation, her late husband's land, and many slaves.

Elisa shared the secret of growing indigo with neighbors. In plantation days, it was common practice for slave owners to rent out their slaves to another slave owner who, for whatever reason, needed extra labor. It seems likely that under Elisa's direction, her slaves showed slaves on other plantations how to grow indigo. Indigo became the third leading, some say the second leading, export for South Carolina.

In 1775, over a million pounds of indigo, worth over thirty million dollars today, got exported to England. Elisa did well financially. However, had she kept the technique of growing indigo to herself, she undoubtedly would have made an even greater fortune. She also would have had fewer friends. When the Revolutionary War broke out, the market for indigo collapsed. During the war, Elisa's sons served as generals in George Washington's Army.

During the conflict, the British burned her plantation. Whether they specifically targeted her plantation because Elisa's sons were generals in the rebel army is unknown.

Elisa Died in 1793. One of her pallbearers was George Washington.

In 1989, nearly two centuries after her death, Elisa became the first woman inducted into the South Carolina Business Hall of Fame.

Mary Kathrine Goddard

Mary Kathrine Goddard was born on June 16, 1738. Her mother came from a wealthy family. Some sources say her father was a doctor. Others firmly report he was a postmaster. He might have been both. Whatever the truth, being born into relative wealth makes it easier, as an adult, to start a business, attend a good college, and buy a home. (Homeownership helps perpetuate wealth to the next generation).

Universal public education and publicly funded colleges, to some extent, offset the benefits of being born into privilege. In America, in the early 18th century, public education at the elementary school level was becoming commonplace. Children were often taught in a one-room schoolhouse, with boys and girls of all grade levels being taught together. However, like other girls in her area, Mary attended school separately from the boys. The girls' school program began after the boys' school day ended.

In 1755, Mary's father became too ill to work. Mary was seventeen years old. To state the obvious, in Pre-Revolutionary America, no social security or disability payments existed. Falling off a horse or other accident could lead to death or incapacitation, so could disease. If the man of the house died or became incapacitated and unable to earn a living, even a well-to-do family could quickly fall into poverty. When Mary's father became seriously ill, too sick to support the family, her older brother William, then fifteen, became a printer's apprentice.

As a young man, William started the first newspaper in Rhode Island, the *Providence Gazette*. Sarah, his mother, and Mary worked in William's family business. William started another newspaper in Baltimore and another newspaper in Philadelphia. William sold the Rhode Island paper and asked his sister and mother to run his newspaper in Philadelphia.

When her mother died in 1770, Mary inherited two papers, the *Maryland Journal* and the *Pennsylvania Chronicle*. However, the newspaper business was not lucrative. Mary sometimes took payment in the flour, meat, lard, and other foodstuffs. Still, she was doing better than her brother. In 1772, unable to pay his debts, William was put in debtor's prison. He would remain there for three years.

A man sent to debtor's prison supposedly could work off his debt by performing useful work. (Only a handful of women have been sent to debtor's prison). A prisoner was usually charged room and board during his incarceration, so his net pay was minimal. Frequently, to be released, a friend or relative had to pay off the man's debt. As Mary was getting paid in meat and lard, it might have taken three years for her to pay her brother's bail. After his release, as there was no national postal system, William started a private mail service.

Through editorials in her newspaper, Mary led a "homespun movement" to boycott British textiles. In 1775, she printed and sold copies of Thomas Paine's *Common Sense*. *Common Sense* formed the intellectual underpinnings of the revolution. That same year, Mary also became the postmaster of Baltimore.

With the declaration of independence in 1776, a Philadelphian named John Dunlap was tasked with printing the Declaration of Independence. He printed two hundred copies. Dunlap printed the declaration without appending the names of the signatories. By omitting the names, which he apparently did on his own initiative, Dunlap sought to protect the lives of the signatories.

Six months later, the Continental Congress commissioned Mary to print additional copies of the Declaration of Independence, thus making Mary the first female government contractor. Mary appended the signatures, which made the document much more powerful. Also, with a dash of self-promotion, she added, "Baltimore in Maryland, printed by Mary Katherine Goddard." When independence came, as she was already serving as a postmaster, Mary was the first female employee in the United States. To supplement her government income, Mary continued her printing business and produced an almanac.

Financially, Mary was doing well. However, with the establishment of a national postal service, William's private mail service was no longer viable. Out of a job, William tried his luck again as a publisher. He retook his role as publisher of the *Maryland Journal*. There is no record that William bought the Maryland Journal from his sister.

Due to a paper shortage and lack of money, he printed the *Maryland Journal* irregularly. It is likely that William usurped his sister's paper simply by printing new issues of the *Maryland Journal* and declaring himself the editor/publisher by putting his name on the masthead.

However, William's betrayal went even further. He also printed an almanac, which put him in direct competition with his sister, and Benjamin Franklin. Mary was furious. When William married, Mary refused to attend the wedding. The siblings would live out their years without ever speaking to each other.

In October 1789, Mary was forced out of the post office business. At the time, postmasters sometimes delivered mail personally, occasionally traveling significant distances. Even though she had been serving as postmaster for several years—it was suddenly decreed such traveling was unsuitable for a woman. Two hundred leading residents of Baltimore, both men and women, protested and signed a petition to have her reinstated. It was to no avail. Still, the men who signed the petition were on the record, saying a woman could do the job—a bold statement given the times. Mary spent the next twenty years running a combination book and dry goods store.

Mary never married and had no children. When she died in 1816 at 78, she left her estate to her servant, Belinda Sterling. The brother who betrayed her got nothing.

Madame Tussaud

Born Marie Grosholtz in Strasbourg in 1761, Madame Tussaud never knew her father. He had died in the Seven Years' War before Marie was born. When Marie was six years old, Marie and her mother moved into the home of a doctor, Phillipe Curtius. Her mother worked as a housekeeper for Dr. Curtius.

Medicine in the last half of the 18th century was relatively primitive. Doctors were still trying to understand basic anatomical functions. To better understand anatomy, some doctors, like Curtius, made wax models of body parts. Likely because he found it more lucrative, Dr. Curtius began using his wax modeling skills for portraits instead of body parts and opened a portrait studio. Like fathers often did with sons, Dr. Curtius made young Marie his apprentice.

Dr. Curtius' wax portrait business prospered, and under his tutelage, in 1777, Marie's first public wax portrait was unveiled. She had done a portrait of Voltaire. To do a portrait of France's best-known scientist was quite an honor. Marie went on to do portraits of the French philosopher Rousseau and America's ambassador to France, Benjamin Franklin. From 1780 to 1789, Marie worked at Versailles as a court artist. While being employed as a court artist was presumably lucrative, when the French Revolution began, having been a court artist was a dangerous job to have on one's resume.

On July 10, 1789, a mob broke into Curtius' studio. (A different mob stormed The Bastille two days later). The mob absconded with wax busts of two political figures believed to be royalists. The mob paraded the wax figureheads, which signified that the mob wanted the political figures guillotined. History doesn't record if the figureheads were made by Curtius or Marie.

The excesses of the French Revolution became known as the Reign of Terror. During the Reign of Terror, Marie was arrested, and her head shaved. A shaved head usually meant the prisoner would soon have an appointment with the guillotine. Dr. Curtius, however, secured Marie's release. Curtius may have secured her release by promising that Marie would use her talents for the rebel cause. Whether in exchange for her release or for other reasons, Marie made death masks of the disembodied heads of Louis XIV, Marie Antoinette, and others.

In 1794, Curtius died. Being the father figure he was to Marie, he willed his substantial collection of wax figures, including the death masks, to Marie. Marie married Francois Tussaud, an engineer, the next year. With her marriage to François, Marie became Madame Tussaud. The couple had two children that survived infancy.

François, however, couldn't find much work as an engineer. Some writers report François' inability to find work stemmed from laziness. While there may be some truth to such an assertion, one must also recognize the political climate. Engineers build bridges, castles, water projects, etc., and construction in such projects can take years. Such projects require political stability and government leaders with a vision for a new bridge, castle, or canal. Had there been political stability, François likely would have made a decent living as an engineer, and Marie's skills with wax would have been more of a side business.

Because of the political volatility, Marie, without François, went to England. She took her wax figureheads with her. Every successful entrepreneur must take risks. Marie did so by opening a museum of her figures. While most of the wax figures were portraits, some were molds of disembodied heads. The macabre display was the predecessor of the House of Horrors, exhibits now seen in Madame Tussaud's wax museums.

The museum proved a great success. Marie was the breadwinner in the family. She did not need the financial or emotional support of her husband. She incorporated her business in such a way so that, in 1850, when she died at the age of 88, her sons, not her husband François, inherited the business.

Today, there are twenty-one Madame Tussaud wax museums worldwide featuring full-sized models of celebrities, actors, and politicians in major cities around the world. The museums are air-conditioned, not just for the comfort of guests and staff, but to help preserve the wax figureheads. (The bodies are made of a special fiberglass)

In 2007, the Tussaud Group sold for 1.7 billion dollars. The wax museums are now owned by Merlin Entertainments. A major corporate shareholder of Merlin Entertainments is Legoland. On Legoland's management webpage, four girls (no boys) are depicted as designers/executives.

Martha Matilda Harper

Martha was born in 1857 in Canada to extremely poor parents. At some point, her family moved with a doctor. In practice, at least at first, she was just a young servant girl. In the last half of the 19th century, the United States had the highest literacy rate in the world, and most girls and boys had at least an elementary school education. As an uneducated servant, Martha's opportunities to find more lucrative employment were minimal. Some sources say, in a parental-like gesture, on his deathbed, her employer, the doctor, gave Martha the formula for a hair tonic. Other sources say that Martha developed the hair tonic herself.

With the death of her employer, Martha became an entrepreneur. She had prudently saved for years. With this start-up money, at the age of thirty-one, Martha opened her first beauty shop. The shampoo she sold and used at her beauty shop was superior to most other shampoos on the market. At the time, some products and tonics were harmful. Martha had beautiful waist-length hair. Her long, beautiful hair was the modern equivalent of a celebrity endorsement.

Martha's first beauty salon was in a prestigious office building in Rochester, New York. One of the other tenants in the building was a children's music studio. The music studio did not have a waiting room, so Martha invited women taking their children to music lessons to wait in her salon. Soon, she was styling hair for the upper-crust society of Rochester.

In the late 1800s, beauty salons and barber shops were uncommon. Most women and men had their hair cut at home by a relative or friend. The well-to-do either had a servant cut their hair, or the stylist came to the home. However, a stylist or barber going from house to house can only cut so much hair in a day.

Martha dubbed the way she styled "the Harper Method." She began opening other salons, which naturally used various Harper products. However, without access to capital to buy new salons, salons using her method were individually owned. Martha had, in essence, developed a new "mousetrap"—the first franchise system.

Martha also developed a reclining chair, making it easier for customers and stylists alike. However, she did not get a patent for her chair. The first barber chair, which did not recline but swiveled, received a patent in 1878.

At its peak, there were five hundred Harper Salons nationwide. Susan B. Anthony, Woodrow Wilson, and Calvin Coolidge had their hair cut with the Harper method.

At age sixty-three, Martha married a man named Robert McBain. Robert was twenty years her junior. Waiting so late in life to get married was a practical business decision. As an unmarried woman, Martha was free to invest in her business, as she felt best. Given the laws then in existence, Martha would have needed her husband's permission to enter contractual obligations.

By marrying a younger man, she had someone to keep the business going once she passed away. The life expectancy for a woman in 1920 was only fifty-three years. As she aged, Robert gradually took over the business. Still, she outlived her husband by a decade and died at ninety-two. By then, almost all her franchises, franchises mostly owned by women, had become fully independent.

Marie Leavue

Marie Leavue was born in New Orleans, Louisiana. Most sources say she was born in 1801. So, she was three years old when the United States purchased Louisiana from France. Marie's mother, Marguerite Darcantre, had been born into slavery but was a free woman and the mistress of Charles Laveaux, a businessman of mixed-race ancestry. Charles acknowledged Marie as his child, but played a minor role in Marie's upbringing.

Louisiana became a state in 1812, the same year America was again at war with Britain. One of the largest battles of the war occurred just outside New Orleans. In 1812, New Orleans was easily the most cosmopolitan city in the United States. There were free-born blacks, like Marie, enslaved blacks, many who had come from French-controlled Haiti, a significant number of mixed-race individuals, and a white population that predominantly spoke French, not English. Also, unlike in the rest of the young nation, Catholicism was the predominant religion.

Many Blacks, free-born or enslaved, blended Catholicism with Haitian/African beliefs, including voodoo. Baptized a Catholic, as an adult, Marie attended mass multiple times a week. However, she also performed voodoo rituals regularly. Whether Marie genuinely believed in voodoo or merely used the pretense of voodoo as part of her scam is unclear.

When she was eighteen, Marie married Jacque Paris. Jacques worked as a cabinetmaker. Marie's father, Charles Laveaux, apparently approved of the marriage and deeded a house he owned to Marie as a wedding present.

While not rich, compared to most Blacks then, Marie was well off. She was a free woman, a homeowner, and her husband had an in-demand job in New Orleans' growing population. However, Jacques died before their second child was baptized. Following common practice, Marie became known as the Widow Paris.

Marie found love again. She lived openly with an affluent white man named Louis Glapion. Interracial marriage was illegal and would remain so even after the Civil War. They had several children, but only two girls survived until adulthood. One surviving daughter they named Marie.

Marie started her commercial involvement in voodoo by selling gris-gris bags. Gris-gris bags had their origins in Muslim practice in West Africa. Originally, a gris-gris bag was a small pouch containing an amulet for luck. Some amulets were touted as a means of birth control. Other amulets were supposed to contain powerful, malevolent spirits and were used to draw misfortune to one's enemies. Gris-gris bags and amulets were just part of the panoply of voodoo. A few decades earlier, in a local revolt, slaves allegedly used the power of gris-gris bags against their owners. Voodoo supposedly influenced the successful slave revolt in 1791 in Haiti. Voodoo was a force that whites respected, even if they didn't understand it.

Marie sold her gris-gris bags at an open market in Congo Square. Congo Square was a meeting place/market for Blacks. During winter and summer solstice, and at other times, events were held in Congo Square. One local newspaper reported that "midnight dances, bathing, and eating, together with less innocent pleasures," occurred during voodoo gatherings in Congo Square. As Marie's lifestyle was substantially better than most Blacks, it was only natural for customers to assume Marie had some powerful magic behind her.

Louis Galpion died in 1855. While she and Louis never married, in practical terms, Marie was a widow again. Selling gris-gris bags brought in only so much money. Fifty-four years old then, she was too old and devout to make a living in the world's oldest profession. In the 19th century, as in the 21st century, a woman without education or job skills can, pun intended, make a respectable amount of money as a prostitute.

In Congo Square, Marie literally put on a song and dance show. Over time, Marie became New Orleans's first "Queen of Voodoo" and, by the standards of the time, became moderately wealthy. The most common explanation for Marie's success is that she and her daughter Marie were hairdressers for the white elite and Blacks affluent to afford a professional haircut. As hairdressers, they learned the gossip around town. With the pretext that the power of voodoo could, for a fee, be employed, they exploited this gossip.

Whatever methods she used, like charlatans everywhere, Marie was convincing. She was as good as any snake oil salesman. Despite the charades, Marie attended mass regularly and continued ministering to the imprisoned.

The police suspected Marie was a fraud. Still, who wants to tempt fate and feel the wrath of the voodoo queen? Further, there was also the political angle. The slave revolt in Haiti was recent history for French-speaking whites in New Orleans. Arresting a very popular voodoo queen could trigger a slave rebellion.

Marie retired as Queen of Voodoo in 1869. Her daughter, sometimes referred to as Marie II, became the new titular head of Voodoo in New Orleans but did not engender the respect accorded to her mother.

The first Marie died in 1881. Her tomb is one of the most visited sites in New Orleans.

The Congo Square continues to be a center of music and celebration for African-Americans. In 2023, the current high priestess in New Orleans is Mambo Sallie Ann Glassman. Glassman is white and of Jewish heritage.

Snake oil salesmen and saleswomen still persist. Elizabeth Holmes claimed to have invented a device that could detect a wide variety of diseases from just a few drops of blood. She bilked investors, many of whom were savvy business people, of over one hundred forty million dollars.

On January 2, 2022, Elizabeth Holmes was convicted of fraud and received an eleven-year sentence.

SCIENTISTS AND SCHOLARS

Introduction:

By the mid-18th century, except for those in slavery, basic literacy for girls and boys was common in North America. In Europe, general literacy came somewhat later. Outside of North America and Europe, illiteracy was common. In the Arab world, even for men, widespread literacy was not common until the latter half of the 20th century.

Geographically, the greater portion of the Arab/Muslim world lies in Asia. Now, in the 21st century, Arab countries that are geographically in Asia have greater than ninety percent literacy for men as well as women—even war-torn Yemen has a literacy rate of over fifty percent for girls. In the Muslim-dominated African countries of Egypt and Libya, over two-thirds of girls can read and write; in Tunisia, it is over ninety percent.

Many non-Arab countries in Asia, such as Japan, Singapore, Taiwan, etc., now have nearly 100 percent literacy for boys and girls. Moreover, students in these countries easily outperform Americans on standardized science and math tests. However, in several non-Arab countries in Africa, such as Niger, Chad, Liberia, etc., less than half of girls and boys are literate.

As North America and Europe had a head start in literacy, most inventions associated with modern living in the 20th century, the airplane, the radio, the transistor, etc., were developed in the West. Products of the 21st century, such as cell phones, high-definition televisions, Blu-Ray players, etc., are manufactured in Asia but developed in North America or Europe. Much of Asia remains under varying degrees of repression. Repressed people do not innovate.

Given the impact of literacy, political repression, and other factors, there are very few female scientists of yesteryear from Africa or Asia. Just two are profiled: Hypatia, who was born in northern Africa but whose ancestry was Greek, and Fatima al-Samarquandi, who was of Arab ancestry but was born in what is modern-day Uzbekistan.

Four female scientists and scholars from Europe and North America are profiled. They are Emilie Du Chatelet, Clara Immerwahr, Henrietta Leavitt, and Heddy Lamar.

Emilie, like almost every literate person in the 17th century, received her education from a tutor. Clara and Henrietta, like the better-known Marie Curie, were in the first wave of women to earn doctorates in the physical sciences.

Heddy Lamar did not earn a doctorate. She didn't even graduate from college. In the 1930s and 1940s, Heddy Lamar was a household name as a sex symbol/movie star. She deserves recognition as she helped develop the technology that led to a very modern invention, the cellphone.

Hypatia

Hypatia's story begins nearly six centuries before her birth, when in 332 B.C., Alexander the Great conquered Egypt. Alexander the Great founded and named many cities for himself, the most famous being Alexandria in Egypt. When Alexander the Great died, one of his generals, Ptolemy, a Greek, began ruling Egypt. Descendants of that first Ptolemy built the famous lighthouse and library of Alexandria. Descendants of Ptolemy ruled Egypt until the death of Cleopatra in 30 B.C. Cleopatra was Greek, not African.

Hypatia was born in 360 A.D., well after the destruction of the famous library and lighthouse. However, Alexandria remained a center of scholarship. Hypatia's father, Theron, was a mathematician, an astronomer, a teacher, and, like many scientists of his time, a philosopher.

In 365 A.D., when Hypatia was five years old, Constantine, the first Christian emperor, convened the Council of Nicaea. The Council of Nicaea standardized Christianity. The Council of Nicaea defined what was canonical (correct) and was not canonical (heresy). As the standardization of time zones helped the expansion of railroads, the standardization of Christian theology helped spread the religion. The ascendency of Christianity, however, had dire consequences for pagans such as Hypatia.

Hypatia followed in her father's footsteps. She was an excellent mathematician, a teacher, and a philosopher. She was particularly well-versed in Plato. In Hypatia's time, books were copied by hand, usually by a lowly scribe who toiled away, copying letter by letter. However, when scholars like Hypatia copied or translated books, they added their own commentaries, and Hypatia was no exception.

Hypatia's most famous work was her translation, including fresh commentaries, of *The Almagest*. For sailors and astronomers, *The Almagest* was the Google Maps of its day. In her commentaries, Hypatia corrected the errors of the men who preceded her. Until the 17th Century, *The Almagest*, with Hypatia's improvements, was the definitive astronomical reference work.

Not surprisingly, virtually all Hypatia's professional relationships were with men. One man, a former student, was Synesius of Cyrene. Syneius became a

Bishop in Libya. As their respective careers progressed, despite their different religions, Cyrene and Hypatia exchanged several friendly letters.

Another colleague was Socrates of Constantinople. Socrates of Constantinople described Hypatia as a woman who has "made such attainments in literature and science as to far surpass all the philosophers of her own time." Socrates of Constantinople went on to observe that Hypatia was self-assured and was at ease speaking in "assemblies" of men. He further opined that "All men admire her extraordinary dignity and virtue."

Hypatia was quite beautiful and had many suitors. However, perhaps valuing her independence more than the need for companionship, Hypatia never married. Reportedly, she was a lifelong virgin.

Theophilus was the governor of the area where she lived. Under his rule, Jews, Pagans, and Christians got along. When Theophilus died, his nephew, Cyril, succeeded him. Cyril was not as broad-minded as his late uncle. Cyril closed all the synagogues and expelled many Jews. He also closed churches that were allied with potential political rivals.

If Cyril was hostile to Jews and some Christians, his attitude towards pagans like Hypatia was worse. Records don't reflect that he singled her out. However, records show, not surprisingly, that she thought little of him.

A Christian mob murdered Hypatia in 415 A.D. It is likely that the mob acted on the orders of Cyril, though some historians believe the mob acted on its own. However, as most of the mob was likely illiterate, someone in the educated elite had to have identified Hypatia as the target.

Fatima al-Samarqandi

Fatima was born in Samarkand during the 12th century. Never heard of Samarkand? Most people haven't. Samarkand was a thriving city in what today is Uzbekistan and was a major "off-ramp" for the Silk Road.

Like Hypatia, Fatima's father was a scholar. Her father wrote an important book on Islamic jurisprudence, and Fatima, at a young age, memorized it. However, Fatima did not merely memorize by rote. She became well-versed in Islamic jurisprudence. Her understanding of Islamic law was considered on par with her father's. Further, sometimes, politely, one assumes, she even corrected her father's Fatwas (religious edicts). Other times, her father would take an issue under advisement and consult with Fatima before issuing a Fatwa.

Fatima also wrote fatwas herself, but they were usually countersigned by her father. In an era before the printing press, fatwas were written out by hand. Fatima's fatwas were admired both for their logic and clarity and for their excellent calligraphy.

Throughout history, men of considerable status and wealth usually have no difficulty finding attractive female companionship. As with Hypatia, many men of considerable wealth and status wanted to marry Fatima. Fatima certainly could have married rich had she wished. Men of status can easily find a pretty woman, but Fatima's suitors obviously wanted something more. They wanted intelligent companionship. However, with her father's blessing, Fatima married for love.

Fatima married Ala al-Din Abu Bakr ibn Massud Kausansani, one of her father's students. The newlyweds moved into her father's home—not the home of her new husband's family. Then, as remains true in much of the Arab world, a newlywed couple, if unable to have their own home, move in with the groom's family. Still, as required by custom, Massud was required to provide a dowry. In his case, it was his eight-volume commentary on a textbook his future father-in-law had written.

Fatima, her husband, and her father later moved to Aleppo. While Baghdad was the heart of Islamic science and intellectual inquiry, provincial capitals like Alexandria and Aleppo were also major centers of scholarship. In

Aleppo, Fatima, her husband, and her father became a trio of experts on Islamic jurisprudence.

Fatima taught her own, presumably all-male classes, in a madrassa or school. To be taught the finer points of Islamic law when one's mother *and father* were likely illiterate must have been quite a cultural shift. Certainly, some of Fatima's students went on to encourage their sons *and daughters* to become well-educated. Their names are lost, but they are part of the march of history.

To help raise scholarship money for her students, Fatima sold bracelets. Fatima died in 1158. For many years after her death, the selling of bracelets for scholarships remained a tradition.

Emilie du Chatelet

Unlike Hypatia and Fatima, Emilie du Chatelet's father was not a scholar or scientist. Her father was a minor noble and first secretary to King Louis XIV. Among other responsibilities as the King's secretary, Emile's father organized weekly get-togethers of France's intellectual elite.

Using his political connections, Emilie's father arranged for the astronomer Bernard Fontenelle to tutor his daughter. He also arranged for other tutors as well. By age twelve, Emilie was fluent in Latin, Greek, and German. However, even for a high-level bureaucrat, paying tutors was a considerable expense. Presumably, the cost could be one reason Emilie's mother opposed her daughter getting such an exemplary education.

As a teenager, to earn extra money, Emilie used her skills in math and developed successful gambling strategies. Also, Emilie, like other young women born into nobility, learned to dance, ride a horse, and play the harpsichord. However, atypically, with her father's backing, Emilie also learned how to fence. As an adult, Emilie translated classical plays written in Greek and Latin into French.

While Emilie's father supported his daughter in becoming an educated and cultured woman, he was not above arranging a marriage for her. At age nineteen, she was married off to a noble by the name of Florent-Claude du Chastellet-Lomont. Emilie was nineteen. Her new husband was thirty-four. Emilie and Lomont had three children, but only one survived past childhood. After her third child, Emilie resumed her studies in mathematics.

One of her new tutors was Alexis Clairaut. Clairaut believed, correctly, that the Earth was not a perfect sphere but bulged in the middle. The science and mathematics involved in demonstrating that the Earth bulges in the middle were well beyond the understating of all but a few of the brightest minds at the time. Clairaut shared his thoughts with no less a figure than Isaac Newton.

Voltaire (from whom we get the word "volt") was a long-time houseguest of Emilie and Lamont. While Voltaire was a houseguest, Emilie published various scientific articles and translations. Emilie also had time for romance. She had an affair with a poet and became pregnant. However, that child did not survive infancy.

Emilie's most famous translation was her translation of Isaac Newton's Principia Mathematica into French. The Principia Mathematica lays out the laws of motion and gravitational attraction. Translating the Principia Mathematic into any language requires a deep understanding of mathematics. Emilie's translation of Principia Mathematica into French is still considered the definitive translation.

Emilie died in 1749 at the relatively young age of forty-two.

Clara Immerwahr

The march of history is framed by decisions large and small. What if Lincoln had not gone to the theater that evening? What if Kennedy's motorcade had taken a different route? Clara Immerwahr did her best to change the course of history but was ultimately ineffective.

Clara was born into a middle-class, educated Jewish family in Germany. Unlike her sisters, Clara was very interested in science. She wanted a career in science like her older brother. However, that path seemed blocked, so she entered a seminary program that taught women how to be teachers. Her female principal gave her a chemistry textbook, which sparked Clara's lifelong interest in the subject.

After taking the required qualifying exam, Clara got permission to attend Breslau University. Initially, like other women, Clara could only audit classes and was not officially enrolled. However, Clara kept on studying. The rules changed, and Clara could pursue a doctoral degree. As Clara's mother, like most women at the time, was a housewife, her father financed her education.

In 1900, Clara was awarded a doctorate in chemistry, the first woman in German to do so. After earning her degree, Clara worked as a laboratory assistant for Professor Richard Abegg. Abegg had supervised Clara's doctoral dissertation.

In 1901, Clara married Fritz Haber, a man she had met several years before at a dancing lesson. Fritz, like Clara, had converted to Christianity some years before. Anti-Semitism was already growing in Germany, and their conversion was more a matter of practicality than faith. Clara and Fritz would have one child, Hermann.

Fritz was an assistant professor of chemistry. Clara collaborated with her new husband in writing a chemistry textbook. In the dedication to the textbook, Fritz wrote, "(to my) beloved wife, Mrs. Clara Haber, Ph.D., with thanks for (her) quiet collaboration."

Fritz and Clara's marriage was not a happy one. Fritz had multiple affairs, and, as his tepid dedication to the textbook indicates, he was not emotionally supportive. Intellectually, Fritz was progressive enough to marry a woman who understood advanced chemistry. Emotionally, he was a man of his times.

In a letter to her former professor, Richard Abegg, Clara vented her frustrations about her husband. How Abegg responded to Clara discussing her marital problems with her former employer/professor is unknown.

Besides helping write her husband's textbook, Clara also gave lectures to women's organizations on chemistry, particularly with respect to household uses. She was not pleased when people assumed her husband had written her lectures.

While he was a poor husband, professionally, Fritz was at the top of his game. He developed a process to synthesize ammonia, a breakthrough for which he would be awarded a Nobel Prize. Developing a process to synthesize ammonia was a major boon for the production of commercial fertilizer. With commercial fertilizer, farms could be much more productive. There were high hopes that, with commercial fertilizer, world hunger could be completely alleviated.

WWI began in 1914. A year later, Fritz volunteered to work for Germany's Supreme War Staff. With his knowledge of chemistry, Fritz came upon the idea of using chlorine gas as a weapon. When Clara learned what her husband had developed, she was thoroughly disgusted. She considered poison gas a "perversion of science." She pleaded with Fritz not to pursue his research.

Fritz ignored his wife's moral objections and continued working on a way to weaponize chlorine. On April 22, 1915, using a method Fritz perfected, Germany launched a gas attack on the Allies. The attack killed hundreds. Fritz was hailed a hero. Clara's disgust only deepened.

On May 2, 1915, in a last-ditch ditched effort to get her husband to cease production and further development of chemical warfare, Clara killed herself. However, her death left Fritz unmoved. He left for military assignment the same day, leaving their son, Hermann, then a teenager, on his own.

Henrietta Leavitt

Henrietta Levitt was born on the Fourth of July in 1858 into a solid middle-class family. Her father was a minister and held a doctorate in divinity. After graduation from high school, Henriette enrolled in Oberlin College, then transferred to the Harvard Annex (which later became Radcliffe). Henrietta earned a B.A. in mathematics and developed an interest in astronomy in her last years in college.

After graduation, Henrietta volunteered for two years at Harvard's Observatory. The Observatory was headed by Edward Pickering. As she didn't have a paying job, her father supported Henrietta. Surely, in her father's pastoral duties, congregants inquired about Henrietta. Explaining that his daughter worked at an observatory likely left many surprised. However, it also opened minds. The march of history has many entrants, both direct and indirect.

In 1902, Henrietta returned to Harvard Observatory. This time as a paid assistant. At the observatory, like the women depicted in the movie *Hidden Figures,* Henrietta and other female assistants were hired, in part, for their ability to perform complex mathematical calculations. Pickering paid Henrietta thirty cents an hour. Some writers have decried her low salary. However, Henrietta's thirty-five cents an hour was a nickel more than the other women in the lab. On a monthly basis, her salary was about that of a schoolteacher.

Henrietta and the other women on Pickering's staff (sometimes jokingly referred to as Pickering's Harem) spent much of their time reviewing photographic plates. Modern astronomy was still in its infancy. Photographic plates took hours to develop. Astronomers compared plates from different nights to make conclusions.

In 1908, Henrietta published a scientific paper titled *1777 Variables in the Magellanic Clouds.* In this paper, Henrietta observed that brighter variable stars (called Cepheid stars) had longer periods of oscillation in relation to their brightness. The distance, luminosity, and periods of oscillation of a few Cepheid stars located "near Earth" were already known by well-established means. Henrietta argued that its brightness and period of oscillation could establish the distance of any Cepheid star. Her conclusion became known as a "standard candle" in astronomy, a nod to the scientific term "foot-candle" as a measure of candle brightness one foot away.

Using Henrietta's "standard candle," Edwin Hubble, for whom the Hubble Space Telescope is named, determined that fuzzy images on photographic plates were galaxies. He correctly concluded that the universe was much larger than anyone had imagined.

Hubble didn't give much credit to Henrietta for her "standard candle" insight, but Leavitt's achievement common knowledge in the small-knit community of astronomers. At least one astronomer thought she deserved a Nobel Prize.

Henrietta's scholarship did not go completely unrewarded. In 1921, she became head of stellar astronomy at Harvard. There is no reference that she was paid less than men holding similar positions. As of this publication, Dr. Lisa Kewley is the director of the Harvard/Smithsonian Center for Astrophysics.

Henrietta, who had often been in ill health, died the same year. Henrietta, like Hypatia, never married and did not have any children.

Heddy Lamar

Heddy Lamar (born Hedwig Eva Kiesler) was born into a well-to-do Jewish family in Vienna on November 9, 1914. Like other upper-class girls of her time, Heddy took piano and ballet lessons. Like the other women profiled in this section, Heddy had a supportive father. Heddy and her father often took walks together. During their walks, they often talked about how things such as streetcars and printing presses worked. Heddy's mother was a concert pianist, an acceptable career for a woman of that era.

Heddy, like Fatima and Hypatia, was quite attractive. As a teen, Heddy got a bit part in her first film. Three movies later, still just eighteen years old, she got the lead female role in the movie *Ecstasy*. The movie poster for *Ecstasy* depicted the face of a woman in (presumably) post-coital bliss. *Ecstasy* was about as sexual as a mainstream movie could get in its day.

As an upcoming young actress, Heddy was doing well for herself. No man her age, just starting his career, would be in her league. Her first marriage, at age nineteen, was to Fritz Mandl, a man fourteen years her senior. Fritz Mandel was a munitions dealer of considerable means. However, Heddy's marriage to Fritz was not happy and produced no children.

After her marriage to Fritz, Heddy moved to London. There she met Hollywood film director David Meyer. She was twenty-four years old. Heddy starred in several major movies, though none were as explicit as *Ecstasy*; Heddy's sexuality oozed on the screen. Being exceptionally attractive, Heddy had her choice of men. In all, Heddy would have six marriages and three children from those marriages. However, only two men, not any of her husbands, supported her scientific side as her father had.

To most of the men of the time, it ran counter to their belief system that women would have careers as scientists. However, to be fair to men, the mothers Emilie du Chatelet and Clara Immerwahr, or the women who attended Clara's lectures, usually held similar beliefs. Belief systems can be changed, but it takes time or overwhelming evidence. When radio was first invented, many Muslim clerics believed radio transmissions were the work of the devil. Their belief system changed only after hearing a radio broadcast where passages from the Quran were recited because, in their belief system, the devil could not quote the Quran.

The two men who supported Heddy Lamar's scientific pursuits were Howard Hughes and George Antheil. Hughes was the Elon Musk of his day, rich, brilliant, and confident, if not arrogant. Hughes and Heddy dated for a while. While most rich men at the time might give their girlfriends a fur coat or a car, Hughes gave Heddy some electronic gear to tinker with. During downtimes on the movie set, Heddy often fiddled with Hughes' gift.

On at least one date, Heddy and Hughes toured one of his aircraft factories. Some women might consider such a date as a man trying to impress a woman. However, for Heddy, it harkened back to the walks she had with her dad. At one point in their relationship, Heddy gave Hughes a design for a new aircraft wing, one based on the anatomy of a fast bird. About the design, Hughes remarked, "You're a genius."

The other supportive man was George Antheil. Antheil was a well-established musician and writer. He had worked with many of the big names in show business. He was married and Heddy's neighbor. When WWII started in Europe, George and Heddy decided to partner up and do something for the war effort. One assumes that George's wife was a secure and confident person herself. Many women would be jealous if their husband was hanging out with one of America's foremost sex symbols.

Using their knowledge of electronics, they thought to design a steerable bomb. Bombs, whether dropped from an airplane, shot from an artillery piece, or a torpedo tube, could not be controlled once launched. It was well understood that radio-controlled bombs were possible, but an enemy could jam a signal, rendering the bomb harmless, or worse, turn the bomb back to its sender. What was needed was a radio system that the enemy could not override.

This is what Heddy and George did. They developed a "switching frequencies" system that could guide a bomb and could not be hacked. That a movie star and a musician could develop a device that gave the United States a decided technological advantage would challenge the belief system of most in the military. To disguise her involvement, Heddy used her married name in the application. Heddy and George were granted a patent in July 1941.

In December 1941, Six months later, Pearl Harbor was attacked. Much of the Navy's surface fleet got destroyed or heavily damaged. Aircraft carriers without the protection from nearby surface vessels make for easy targets. The defense of Hawaii and the West Coast would rely heavily on submarines. However, torpedoes were notoriously unreliable. They often ran too deep or failed to explode. A steerable torpedo would have been a very useful weapon.

About the time Heddy and George got their patent, Heddy divorced her husband, Gene Markey. She and Gene had been married only two years. One wonders if Heddy's close relationship with George had something to do with the divorce. After all, if Heddy told her husband something like, "I'm off to design a steerable bomb with George," such a statement would run counter to Gene's belief system.

Like George, Gene was a "Hollywood Man" and wrote and produced several movies. George had served in the Navy in WWI. When he re-enlisted for WWII, Gene went into the service as a Lieutenant Commander. He quickly rose through the ranks and retired as an admiral.

Gene never commanded submarines, but served on the staff of very influential officers. He was in a position to promote his ex-wife's patent, but apparently did not do so. In this author's opinion, it required too much cognitive refocusing for Gene to accept that his actress-wife and her musician friend could develop a radio system that the Navy could not. One wonders if Heddy Lamar had married Howard Hughes instead of Gene Markey, if steerable bombs would have hastened the end of the war.

After divorcing Markey, Heddy married a British actor, John Loder. She had three children with him, the first while she was still married to Gene Markey. Heddy and Loder divorced in 1947.

In the 1950s, Heddy starred in several movies and won critical acclaim, but she was not the sex symbol of her youth. She made her last movie in 1958. There were also no more patents or new wing designs.

Heddy's last marriage lasted just two years and ended in 1965. If Heddy had married and stayed with Hughes, it might have been a good marriage for both. Hughes lived out the last years of his life as a recluse. Heddy lived out the last years of her life, spending hours on the phone.

Twice in her retirement years, even though she still had plenty of money, Heddy was caught shoplifting. Psychologically, shoplifting can be a plea for attention. By then, her relationship with Hughes was long over and George had died in 1959. Further, she had been estranged from one child since his teen years.

Perhaps also a plea for attention, Heddy filed a lawsuit against the publisher of her autobiography, claiming the ghostwriter had taken liberties with the truth. She also filed a defamation lawsuit again Mel Brooks. She felt offended by the "Hedley Lamar" character in Brooks' hit movie *Blazing Saddles*.

Because of the technology Heddy developed with George, some writers have mistakenly hailed Heddy Lamar as the grandmother of GPS. This claim shows a complete misunderstanding of the scientific principles involved. GPS was developed by the US military. GPS stands for Global *Positioning* System. It is a distinct technology from the technology of "switching frequencies" that allows hundreds of cell phones to use the same cell phone tower simultaneously.

Heddy Lamar died in 2014 at the age of eighty-five. By then, nearly eighty percent of US households had cell phones.

SPIES

85

Introduction:

Spies have been part of warfare since the beginning of civilization. In modern times, because of their use of subterfuge, spies, unlike prisoners of war, can, according to the Geneva Convention, be lawfully executed.

The ideal spy is someone who, by their looks, demeanor, or status, can remain "hidden in plain sight." We will see how, in "yesteryear," because of prevailing attitudes, female spies could "hide in plain sight."

Our first example, taken from the Revolutionary War, is that of Lydia Barrington Darragh. Lydia was a Quaker, a pacifist. Both because she was a woman and a pacifist, the enemy felt comfortable conducting meetings in her home.

Our second example concerns two women, Elizabeth Van Lew, and Mary Bowser. Elizabeth Van Lew's parents were well-to-do, and Mary had been a slave in her parent's household. Elizabeth's status as an upper-crust lady sheltered her from suspicion. As a Black woman, Mary was assumed to be illiterate, unintelligent, and therefore utterly unqualified in the eyes of Confederates to be a spy.

The most well-known spy of WWI was Mata Hari. The French military employed her to ferret out double agents. Her efforts at seduction were successful, but her efforts in turning seduction into actionable intelligence were not. The notion of female spies using their seductive ways to "loosen lips" is the stuff of fiction. Your author is unaware of any occasion where a bona fide female spy of any nation used seduction to obtain secrets. (However, in the 1980s, a male Chinese spy, pretending to be a woman, successfully obtained several documents from a French diplomat).

After WWI ended, Mata-Hari was arrested for being a spy for Germany. Her trial was front-page news for days. At her trial, Mata Hari readily admitted she was a "harlot" but denied spying for Germany. Despite little in the way of evidence, she was found guilty. Mata was Hari executed on October 15, 1917. The most effective female spy in WWI was Louise Marie de Bettignies, a name unknown to most.

The most effective, most well-known, and most decorated spy in WWII was Virginia Hall. Virginia's life formed the basis of the 2019 film *A Woman of*

No Importance. Virginia tried to become a diplomat, but because of a hunting accident, she walked with a limp. Having a limp disqualified her from serving in the military or the State Department. Initially, having a limp allowed Virginia to hide in plain sight. Spies are supposed to blend in. Someone with an obvious limp is easily noticed; hence, the natural assumption is that the person with the limp can't be a spy. It takes cognitive refocusing to break that assumption.

However, we'll consider two lesser-known female spies from WWII, Aline Griffith and Ursula Kuczynski. Ursula "hid in plain sight" in China, Switzerland, Manchuria, and the UK. Aline spied on Germans in neutral Spain. She was very visible and mixed with Spanish high society. High-society women don't fit the profile of a spy.

In modern times, some women want careers in the military or as spies. Historically, it has been men who went off to war. If he had children, the children stayed behind with the mother. When a woman with children goes off to serve her country either as a soldier or spy and leaves the children with the father, where does he fit in society? Would he be teased by his buddies for being hen-pecked? Ursula Kuczynski's first husband was such a man.

Lydia Barrington Darragh

Lydia Barrington Darragh was forty-seven years old when the Revolutionary War began. Her husband, William Darragh, was ten years her senior. William worked as a private teacher. Lydia and her siblings had been some of William's students.

Lydia and William had nine children. Four died in infancy. Between her duties as wife and mother, Lydia was also a midwife. Financially, Lydia and William must have done fairly well. They and their children lived in a two-story home in Philadelphia. The Darraghs lived in a good neighborhood. While there are exceptions, spies usually come from the affluent, educated class.

During the Revolutionary War, the British captured Philadelphia. As the British came in, many civilians evacuated the city. Breaking with the notion of "women and children first," William and some of his children were part of this exodus and Lydia stayed behind with the other children. With troops literally in her neighborhood, Lydia (and anyone else) could observe the strength of Howe's troops. Some sources say that after her city was occupied by the British, Lydia used her teenage son to ferry messages to the Continental Army.

General William Howe commanded the British in Philadelphia. Like any good general, Howe needed to discuss future battle plans with his officers. To General Howe, Lydia's nice home looked like a great place to hold staff meetings. Lydia was hiding in plain sight in her own home.

Sources disagree on some of the particulars of Lydia's espionage. However, there is wide agreement that on the evening of December 2, 1777, General Howe held a particularly important meeting in Lydia's home. While Howe held his meeting, Lydia was upstairs in bed, supposedly asleep. Lydia, though, remained awake and overheard Howe's plans. She learned of an ambush they planned.

The next day, likely using the pretext that she needed flour, Lydia got permission to pass through British lines. She made contact with an American soldier and informed him of the ambush. The soldier took her observations seriously and forwarded them up the chain of command. That the soldier accepted her word suggests that Lydia was already known to American officers.

Based on the information Lydia provided, the Continental Army avoided the ambush. Because of her efforts in the war, Lydia and her husband were excommunicated from the Quaker church.

Except for her short stint as a spy, Lydia lived a lifestyle that was typical of women of her era. She had several children. Presumably, most of her day was filled with child-rearing and household chores.

In 1783, Lydia's husband, William, died. Lydia lived another six years. Despite being excommunicated, they were buried next to each other in a Quaker cemetery.

Elizabeth Van Lew and Mary Bowser

Elizabeth Van Lew was born in 1818 into an affluent family in Richmond, Virginia. Like other affluent families in Richmond, the Van Lews owned slaves.

Elizabeth was twenty-five years old when her father, John Van Lew, died. This left Elizabeth and her mother, Eliza Van Lew, in charge of the plantation and several slaves. John's will, like many wills at the time, contained a "do not emancipate" clause. Legally, the widow could not emancipate the slaves she now owned. However, she could sell them. Some widows defied the law and freed their slaves. Most sources agreed that Eliza Van Lew granted manumission for the slaves her husband had purchased. Other sources add that to prevent families from being separated, Eliza bought and then freed many other slaves.

One slave John Van Lew owned before his death, was a girl named Mary. Mary held a special place in the family. She was baptized in the Van Lew family church, though almost certainly not during a regular church service. (As a side note, over a hundred years later, Martin Luther King remarked that Sunday morning was America's most segregated time of the week).

Unlike slaves in the Roman Empire, in the American South, it was illegal to educate slaves, even if they were sent to a free state. Elizabeth defied the law and arranged for Mary to be educated in the North. Some years later, when Mary was just fourteen, through the American Colonization Society, Eliza and her mother arranged for Mary's passage to Liberia.

Many, if not most, of the members of the American Colonization Society felt sending former slaves to Liberia was the Christian thing to do. Mary was one of the nearly 20,000 freeborn Blacks and former slaves sent to Liberia to start new lives. To this day, the Liberian flag bears an obvious resemblance to the American Flag.

Mary was not happy in Liberia and returned to the United States. One wonders how her return passage came about. Perhaps a ship's captain or other official felt it their Christian duty to help repatriate Mary to America. It is also plausible that as a teenager and a Black girl traveling alone, she may have had to buy passage with her body. However she secured her passage, Mary rejoined Elizabeth Van Lew and Elizabeth's mother, Eliza Van Lew.

Soon after Mary returned to the Van Lew plantation, Elizabeth was arrested for arranging for Mary to be educated. Elizabeth remained in jail for ten days until her mother paid her bail. Four days before the Civil War broke out, Mary married a man named Wilson Bowser, a servant of the Van Lew family.

The North, with superior numbers of soldiers, cannons, and warships, was fully expected to win the war easily. However, the South put up more resistance than expected. In the first Battle of Manassas, 900 Union soldiers died—the highest death toll for a battle until that time. As the war continued, the Confederacy housed thousands of Union prisoners of war in a warehouse that became known as Libby Prison.

Much to the consternation of their neighbors, Elizabeth Van Lew provided much-needed aid and comfort to the prisoners. Some sources say that from contact with union prisoners, Elizabeth gathered intelligence about the South. However, it is doubtful that captured Union soldiers knew about more Confederate plans than was likely already known by Union commanders.

Elizabeth and her mother continued their humanitarian assistance to the Union soldiers. They secured the transfer of sick prisoners to a hospital where they could receive better food. Malnutrition, especially towards the end of the war, was common in Confederate prisons. In December 1863, with Elizabeth Van Lew's help, two officers escaped. The two officers subsequently vouched that Elizabeth could be trusted.

Acting on the officers' recommendation, General Benjamin Butler began using Elizabeth as a Union spy. Using invisible ink, a code, and trusted messengers, Elizabeth relayed information about troop movements and other intelligence to commanders on the Union side.

Elizabeth became a spymaster herself. Soon, Elizabeth had several agents, the most important of which was Mary. The Confederate White House was located just miles from the Van Lew plantation. Some sources state that Mary found work as a servant in the Confederate bastion. While there is no direct evidence that Mary worked in the Confederate White House, few other locations would have provided the high-level intelligence she gathered.

Mary's natural vocabulary and manner of speech would have been distinct from the other house slaves. She had been educated in the north and lived in Liberia. She would have had to watch her words carefully. This author speculates some staff noticed the difference and helped maintain the ruse. Undoubtedly, Mary was the only one who could read and write.

Exactly how or what military information Mary obtained has been lost to history. She may have gathered her intelligence by listening to Jefferson Davis conferring with his generals or by rifling through his desk to look over maps and correspondence, or both.

However, gathering intelligence is only half of a spy's job. The other part, sometimes just as hard, is getting that intelligence back to someone who can use it. Some sources say that Mary used a basket of eggs with a false bottom to get her intelligence to Elizabeth. Whatever methods they employed, General Grant found the information most useful.

After the war, Grant personally thanked Elizabeth Van Lew for her efforts and backed up his thanks with some cash. Mary didn't get any credit or money. Your author speculates that Elizabeth didn't tell Grant about Mary because she wanted to protect her. As a white woman who supported the South, Elizabeth would be ostracized for the rest of her life. If a Southerner learned that a former slave had been a key Union spy, Mary's fate could have been much worse.

After the war, tens of thousands of men were out of work. The South's economy was at a standstill. Food was scarce. When Grant became President in 1869, Elizabeth worked as the local postmaster. Civil service system rules were decades away. Patronage appointments, like that of postmaster, were commonplace. The appointment was clearly a reward for her service to the union effort. However, appointing a woman to a government position, when so many men were out of work, was a bold move.

When McKinley was elected President, Elizabeth lost her patronage job. By then, Elizabeth was in her seventies. She had no children to support her. She turned to the grandson of Paul Revere and other Northerners to support her financially until she died in 1900.

Mary, Elizabeth's top spy, was about twenty-three years old when the Civil War ended. Many newly freed Blacks had no other option but to continue working in the fields, but Mary, being literate, had options. She separated from her husband.

The years after the Civil War are known as the Reconstruction Era. One of the major programs of the day was the Freedman's Bureau. The Freedmen's Bureau was created to uplift the lives of newly freed Blacks. With money from Washington, agents of the Freedmen's Bureau built numerous schools and several hospitals and established three universities (Howard, Fisk, and Hampton) for Blacks, including a handful of Black women. Now, a Black woman is much more likely to be a college graduate, a doctor, a psychologist, or a lawyer than a Black man.

With her northern education, Mary might have attended college. However, with help from the Freedman Bureau, she established a school. In separate programs, the school taught children and adults. However, after a few years, Mary was told to close the school. One can surmise they directed her to close the school out of concern for the students' safety. Mary's long association with Elizabeth Van Lew, an acknowledged spy for the union, put her and her students' lives at risk from Confederate sympathizers.

Whether it was because of a concern for the students' safety, or other reasons, the school was closed after a few years. Mary then went on a lecture circuit. For her personal safety, she used various aliases. In 1867, while on the lecture circuit, Mary met Harriet Beecher Stowe, and the two exchanged stories.

Also, in 1867, Mary wrote at least two letters to her boss at the Georgia Superintendent of Education. In one letter, she informed the Superintendent that she had married, and her new husband was in Cuba. Other accounts mention the West Indies. In the second letter, she demanded her back pay. From there, Mary disappears from history.

Louise Marie de Bettignies

Louise Marie de Bettignies was born in 1880 in northern France. She was one of eight children. Her family tree could be traced back to the 1200s. The family, for generations, had been in the porcelain-making business, and royal families were their customers. However, the "age of Kings" was fast disappearing, and so was the demand for porcelain. Her family ancestry was old money, but her parents were of modest means. Despite their modest economic status, the family retained its heritage of high culture. Louise's mother and father made sure that Louise received a good education. Louise became fluent in English, German, and Italian and spoke some Russian and Czech as well.

Educated but financially strapped young women like Louise filled a niche in the labor market. They were hired as private tutors or governesses by upper-class families. While by today's standards, hiring a governess or a tutor seems snobbish in an era before immunizations and antibiotics, keeping one's children distant from the masses was also a practical matter of keeping one's children safe.

Louise served as a governess for several years but switched employers frequently. Why did she change jobs so frequently? One can only speculate. Maybe a duke or a baron or two wanted something more than just a teacher for her children. Or maybe she changed jobs frequently as she wanted to see the world. Maybe both. Being a traveling governess was one way for a young woman to have some adventure.

On July 28, 1914, the Archduke of Austria was assassinated, and WWI began. By December 1914, Louise was back in northern France. She and her sister aided the French war effort by getting supplies to men defending the city. Louise was thirty-four, well past the age women typically married.

Louise was reluctant to become a spy. It took three men to persuade her to do so. The first man was a French military officer, but she politely declined. The second man, a British officer, at least got her to consider the idea. It was only after a third man, a priest, supported the idea that she agreed to become a spy.

Louise not only became a spy but a spymaster. At one point, Louise had eighty spies working under her direction—an unusually large number for any spymaster. Even though she was supervising others, Louise continued to collect intelligence personally. When she did so, she often buddied up with her friend, Marie-Léonie Vanhoutte.

Louise went by the code name of Alice Dubois. Alice Dubois and her network gathered much information, including precious, actionable intelligence. In particular, Louise learned the time and route of the Kaiser's train. Based on that information, the train was attacked, but the assault was unsuccessful. Louise and her network learned of Germany's planned assault on Verdun. However, for reasons which are unclear, this information never made its way up to top commanders. Over 160,000 French soldiers died at Verdun, along with a slightly smaller number of German soldiers.

Some sources imply that Louise was ignored because she was a woman. However, as her intelligence about the Kaiser's train had been spot on, this is unlikely. Her intelligence might been ignored because it was never delivered. In WWI, radio communication was still in its infancy and often messages were hand-delivered. To get a message through the chain of command to the main headquarters, many hands and radio operators would have been involved. Ordinary human error, not sexism, is the most likely explanation for the breakdown in communication.

On September 14, 1915, the Germans arrested Louise's friend Marie. Most spies were tortured. Perhaps because she was a woman, Marie was interrogated instead. Her interrogators duped her into revealing her boss's identity. Weeks later, Louise was arrested while trying to cross the border back to France.

In March 1915, Louise was sentenced to death. However, like with her friend Marie, some chivalry was involved, and her sentence was commuted to life imprisonment. (Marie was sentenced to fifteen years). In 1917, while in custody, Marie helped lead a prisoners' revolt. The revolt was not successful, and Marie was put in solitary confinement. On September 27, 1918, Marie died in prison from pleurisy. She was buried in Cologne.

Posthumously, Marie was awarded the Croix de Guerre and the Order of the British Empire. After the war, her remains were repatriated to France. On February 21, 1921, she was reburied in her native country. Several streets in France are named in her honor.

Louise never married. It is plausible she might have been asexual or gay, but given her traditional religious beliefs, she did not permit herself to express her sexuality. For decades, using a polygraph, the CIA routinely asked applicants and employees about their sexual orientation. This was not anti-gay bias per se, but the fear was that agents could be blackmailed into revealing secrets.

Aline Griffith

Aline Griffith was born in 1923 in Pearl River, a very small town in upstate New York. WWII had started by the time Aline graduated high school. After graduation, at her parents' insistence, Aline attended Mount Saint Vincent, a Catholic college for women in New York City. Aline's two older brothers, like millions of other men, skipped college and enlisted.

After college, Aline began working as a model for the Hattie Carnegie model agency. Hattie Carnegie, no relation to Andrew Carnegie, one of the richest men in America. Hattie assumed his last name and developed a very successful modeling agency.

Hattie socialized in the upper crust of society. She invited Aline to several dinner parties. During one party, Aline became acquainted with a man named Frank Ryan, though that was not the name he used. Frank worked for the Office of Strategic Services, the precursor to the CIA.

Frank told Aline he might have a job for her in the War Department and she should expect a call from a certain Mr. Tomlinson. Weeks passed, and finally, "Mr. Tomlinson" called. He asked Aline to meet him in the lobby of a certain hotel the next day. (Times were so innocent then). As they had never met, just like in a classic spy movie, Mr. Tomlinson directed Aline to look for a man with a carnation in his lapel.

The meeting went well, and Aline was hired. Like other recruits, Aline was sent to "the farm" to learn spycraft. Once she completed her training, she was flown to Spain. Only the most important traveled by plane; even high-ranking officers went by ship. Frank was important enough and valued Aline enough to arrange for her to go by air.

Aline's cover was that she worked for the State Department monitoring oil sales by neutral Spain. In reality, she was a cipher clerk, intercepting and decoding enemy messages. She had a regular shift and technically was always on call, in practice, most of her evenings were free.

Madrid had a vibrant nightlife, and Aline particularly enjoyed watching Flamenco dancing. Frequenting Madrid's many nightclubs, Aline soon drew the attention of Juanito Belmonte, Spain's most famous bullfighter. Aline found bullfighting disgusting and was reluctant to date Juanito. However, with his old-world charm, he gradually won her over. On one date with Juanito, with a practice bull, Aline even tried wielding the cape herself.

Aline's relationship with Juanito gained her entrance into the upper crust of Spanish society, including Spanish royalty. Aline was a guest at A-list events. Some events included overnight stays at castles or on large estates.

Politically, Spain's upper crust was divided. Some were sympathetic to allies, some were sympathetic to the Nazis, and a few were actual Nazi operatives. What Aline learned and saw at dinner parties and elsewhere became more important than her cipher duties. Soon Aline was a full-fledged spy herself and, not soon after that, recruited her own spies.

In her espionage, Aline frequently partnered up with Edmundo Lassalle, a major executive with the Walt Disney Corporation. She and Edmundo mixed business with pleasure and dined at some of Madrid's best restaurants. While they dined and otherwise enjoyed Madrid's nightlife, Aline and Edmundo did not get romantically involved. He pinned for a German princess, whose political sympathies were presumed to be pro-Nazi, but Edmundo believed otherwise.

Socializing in the best restaurants, clubs, and elsewhere, however, required nice clothes. Aline frequented one of the best dress shops in Madrid. Aline could afford to be well-dressed as her government salary went far in Spain. However, after some investigation, Aline learned the dress shop was also a Nazi front company. She had the owner put under surveillance.

In addition to traditional spycraft, the OSS in Spain was charged with spiriting French partisans to safety. These partisans, often by foot, made the long journey from France over the Pyrenees into neutral Spain. On short notice, Aline was told to make her apartment available as a safe house for two female partisans. After days of trekking over the Pyrenees, the women were thrilled to have good food, a warm place to stay, and a host that spoke excellent French! The next morning, as usual, Aline went to the embassy.

When she returned from work, Aline found the two partisan women dead in her apartment. They had been murdered either by German spies or, more likely, Nazi sympathizers. Aline could not call the police about the murders. Just like the elite, some ordinary Spaniards favored the Allies; others were Nazi sympathizers. If she contacted the police, word of the murder of two women in an American's apartment would spread. Aline couldn't risk further exposure.

With the help of others from the OSS office, the bodies of the two women were removed from the apartment, and Aline found a new place to stay.

As the war came to a close, the duties of her OSS assignment changed. She and other agents were tasked with preventing Nazis from fleeing Spain and taking whatever wealth, which included art, they had accumulated. Aline also quit dating the bullfighter and began dating Luis De Figueroa, a count in the Spanish Nobility.

Luis came from old money, and his politics were decidedly pro-allied. She and Luis dined, golfed, and otherwise enjoyed the good life. Aline fell in love with Luis and felt the feeling was mutual. Aline expected he would propose to her any day.

When the war ended, Madrid's OSS office closed. Most agents were eager to return to the United States. As Luis had not proposed, Aline, undoubtedly, considered returning to New York, see her family, and settle down with some nice guy. However, Frank had offered her a job at a CIA front company in Paris. Aline still wanted adventure and accepted the job. On learning Aline would be working in Paris, Luis sent *several dozen* flowers to her apartment, but still did not propose. Aline kept her promise to Frank and started her new job.

As in Madrid, Aline enjoyed the Parisian nightlife. With Luis seemingly out of her life, Aline went out with several men. Of course, enjoying the nightlife meant more new clothes. To buy some new outfits, Aline went to one of the high-end dressmakers in France. The dressmaker asked Aline to do a photo shoot to promote a new dress line. Aline was reluctant to return to modeling. However, Frank particularly liked the idea because if Aline had legitimate work, it helped maintain her cover.

Wanting to keep options open, Aline had continued paying rent on her apartment in Madrid. Her former housekeepers picked up her mail and otherwise looked after the apartment. Alice informed the housekeepers she would be returning to Madrid for a short vacation. Without telling Aline, the housekeepers informed Luis of Aline's return to Madrid. When she arrived at her apartment, Luis had again arranged the delivery of many flowers.

Aline and Luis dated much as before, even so, Luis did not propose. Aline couldn't keep Frank waiting; she had to get back to her job in Paris. The night before her departure, Aline told Luis she was having dinner at a certain restaurant with Raimundo Lanza, an Italian prince. As a spy, Aline was used to using people. She used Raimundo to force Luis to propose or have him understand she would start dating other men. The ploy worked. While Aline and Raimundo were having dessert, Luis came to their table. Demonstrating his sincerity by having his father and a priest nearby, Luis asked Aline to marry him.

When Luis proposed, Aline, of course, said yes. She cabled her resignation to Frank. With her marriage to Luis, Aline became part of Spanish royalty. Aline and Luis took a year-long honeymoon in Europe and the United States. They visited her hometown.

Aline and Luis had an exceptionally happy marriage. Aline and Luis were part of high society. They counted many movie stars and royalty among their friends. In 1962, Aline was inducted into *Vanity Fair's* International Best-Dressed Hall of Fame high society.

Aline still took occasional jobs for the CIA. According to one biographer, Larry Loftis, she never told Luis about these side jobs. With his old-world manners, Aline knew Luis probably would not approve of her continuing in espionage; even good marriages have some secrets.

Aline wrote multiple books about her days in the OSS. Declassified material corroborates much but not all her accounts. Luis died in 1987. Aline lived another twenty years. She never remarried.

Aline had close but professional relationships with many men, but especially with Frank Ryan. Nowadays, lest rumors start, many women, as well as their male supervisors, are reluctant to form such intimate relationships. Some corporations even have no fraternizing rules that even apply to consenting adults outside of boss/subordinate situations. In his autobiography, Barack Obama acknowledged that in today's corporate culture, he would never have asked Michelle out.

Unless issues of national security are at stake, the government stays out of the bedroom. If Uncle Sam stays out of the bedroom, what gives the human resources department in corporate America to say the "Barack Obamas" in this world that they can't find their "Michelles?"

Ursula Maria Kuczynski (aka Agent Sonya)

Ursula was born in Berlin on May 14, 1907. Her family was Jewish, but not particularly observant. Berlin in the early 20th century had a large Jewish population, perhaps, as many as 160,000 persons. Jewish families like Ursula's were prominent in the city's intelligentsia. Her family was wealthy enough to have several servants.

Ursula's father, Ollo Kuczynski, was a prominent mathematician. One of his father's closest friends was Albert Einstein. Dinner guests in the Kuczynski household included many prominent Jews and Gentiles, and dinner table conversation often focused on politics. Most attendees were left-leaning, some even communists. While Ursula's father was a wealthy man, Ollo had a good heart. At the dinner table and elsewhere, he spoke up about the wretched conditions of Germany's slums.

Ursula's mother, Berta Kuczynski, had trained to become a dancer but never made dancing a career. She was also not much of a stay-at-home mother, either. She left much of the child-rearing of Ursula and her siblings to a nanny, Olga.

During WWI, the family's fortunes declined. Most of the servants were let go, but Olga, the nanny, remained. In a butterfly fly flapping its wings moment of history, had the nanny been dismissed with the rest of the servants, the course of history might have been dramatically changed.

Ursula wanted to attend college. While her parents were liberal in most respects, college, in their opinion, was for sons, not daughters. At her mother's insistence, at age sixteen, Ursula learned typing and shorthand. In her mother's eye, Ursula needed practical skills. Being able to type and do shorthand, Ursula could get a job as a secretary.

Just short of her seventeenth birthday, Ursula took part in a May Day parade organized by the communist party. During the parade, a cadre of brown-shirted fascists did not like what the communists were saying, and a violent clash broke out. A police officer's truncheon hit Ursula, and she fell to the ground. A friend helped her to her feet, and despite being in pain, Ursula continued taking part in the demonstration. When she got home, while sympathetic to their daughter's politics, Ursula's parents were angered that she had put herself in danger.

Soon after the parade, Ursula met Rudi Hamburger. They dated seriously. Still, Ursula wanted to see the world before settling down with Rudi, so she left for the United States. In New York, Ursula worked part time for Lillian Wald. Wald operated an agency that provided services to immigrants and promoted racial and gender equality. Also, while in New York, Ursula joined the American Communist Party. Ursula would remain a communist for the rest of her life.

In addition to working for Wald, Ursula worked in a bookstore that catered to a liberal clientele. Through her work at the bookstore, Ursula became acquainted with the writings of feminist Agnes Smedley. Years later, on the other side of the world, Ursula and Agnes became what today we would call frenemies.

In 1929, the stock market crashed, and Ursula returned to Germany. The Great Depression put millions of Americans out of work and hit Germany even harder. Still, despite the hard times, Ursula and Rudi married. Rudi had recently qualified as an architect. However, like François Tussaud and the French Revolution, in the Great Depression, there were few jobs needing architects. A childhood friend of Rudi's offered him a job working for the German firm Siemens in Shanghai. Ursula and Rudi, via Moscow, took trains to Shanghai. They did not have enough money for a return ticket.

At the time, Shanghai was China's largest city. Fifty thousand foreigners lived in various enclaves called concessions. Some of the most beautiful buildings in the city were in British and French concessions. Because of concessions granted from the Opium War, Europeans were largely immune from Chinese law. Rickshaws were still common in the city, along with corruption and vice. Police authority was heavy-handed. A little after Rudi and Ursula's arrival, there was a mass arrest of communists, and hundreds were killed.

Rudi's job paid well, and the newlyweds could afford to hire servants. Ursula led what communists would call the bourgeois lifestyle. As expected of someone in their situation, Rudi and Ursula entertained regularly. However, Ursula grew tired of the cocktail and dinner parties and being a housewife. She was also tired of Shanghai's oppressive heat. It didn't help that she was pregnant.

To do something beyond attending boring parties, Ursula began working for a Chinese news agency. Through her well-connected boss, she met Agnes Smedley, the writer she so much admired when Ursula was in New York. Agnes secretly worked for the Comintern (the international communist party) and the fourth directorate, a branch of Soviet military intelligence.

Agnes introduced Ursula to a man named Richard Sorge. Both in looks and manner, he was like the fictional James Bond. He was handsome, adept as a spy, and quite a womanizer. Richard and Agnes were lovers, but not a committed couple. Ursula and Richard were too bohemian to be exclusive.

On February 7, 1931, another mass arrest of Chinese communists occurred. Five days later, Ursula gave birth to a boy. She named the child Michael after a man she had met while in New York. Ursula expected, at least for a while, to be a stay-at-home mom with her new baby. Richard, however, had other plans for her. He actively recruited Ursula to join his spy ring. He correctly reasoned that a woman with a small child could "hide in plain sight."

As part of his effort to groom Ursula into espionage, he took Ursula on a long motorbike ride. (Your author assumes that while Ursula off riding with Richard, her husband was at work, and her young son was in the care of a servant). In Richard, Ursula was finding the excitement she wanted. She and Richard soon became lovers. When Agnes learned that Richard and Ursula were lovers, the relationship between the two women chilled considerably.

At Richard's request, Ursula allowed Richard to use her home for covert meetings during the day while Rudi was at work. To his Soviet handler, Richard gave Ursula the code name, "Sonya," a code name that would be hers for the rest of her career in espionage. Ursula did not tell Rudi that their home was being used for clandestine meetings. Rudi and Ursula continued to entertain at their home regularly. An array of Shanghai's Whose Who, including Richard Sorge, were guests. Dinner table conversation naturally turned to politics.

On June 15, 1931, Chinese authorities arrested Soviet operatives Hiliare and Gertrude Noulens. The Noulens had spent over a hundred thousand dollars of Russia's money to further the communist party in Asia. Because of the Noulens' arrest, Agnes became the guardian of their child.

Ursula feared arrest and worried about what might happen to her young child, but she still did Richard's bidding for the communist cause. Richard asked Ursula to hide a comrade wanted by the police in her home for a few days. Ursula now had to come clean to Rudi about how she had been helping Richard.

Rudi was sympathetic to the communist cause. Back home in Germany, vandalism against Jewish-owned businesses was commonplace. Rudi firmly believed that only the communists could challenge the Nazi party. However, he balked at harboring a fugitive. Ursula defied her husband and did as her lover and comrade asked and hid the fugitive. This angered Rudi, but, for the sake of their child, he did not ask for a divorce.

On January 28, 1932, Japan seized Shanghai. Japanese forces were careful not to attack the international concession, so foreigners were relatively safe. Still, Richard Sorge wanted details of the attack and dispatched Ursula to observe the situation. She did not obtain any actionable intelligence. However, when she found a dead baby in the street. It horrified her; Mike, her first child, was just a toddler himself.

Soon after the attack on Shanghai, Richard was recalled to Moscow. Agnes soon followed. With her closest friend and her lover in Russia, fearing for her child's safety and the Japanese advancing, Ursula knew she and her family had to leave Shanghai.

Because Ursula and her husband were Jewish and, with the Gestapo now fully in charge back home, returning to Germany was out of the question. Ursula and Rudi made their way to his parents in seemingly safe Czechoslovakia. However, for reasons which are not clear, Rudi returned to Shanghai. Ursula then went to Moscow for further training in spycraft, leaving young Michael with Rudi's parents.

Ursula learned that for her next assignment, her new boss would be a thirty-four-year-old Lithuanian named Johann Patra. Unlike her husband Rudi, her lover Richard, or her sometimes friend Agnes, Johann was no intellectual. He could barely read and write. He was a rugged, handsome outdoor kind of guy and spoke multiple languages.

Johann and Ursula learned they would be posted in Manchuria. One of the main objectives of their assignment would be to set up a clandestine radio. After the meeting at headquarters, at Johann's suggestion, he and Ursula met for dinner to further discuss the assignment. After dinner, they went to a movie. The business meeting turned into a date. On route to Manchuria, Ursula and

Johann picked up Ursula's now three-year-old son, Michael, in Czechoslovakia. Michael took a while to warm up to his mother.

Johann's cover was that he was an executive for a typewriter company. However, the rugged man that he was, he needed pointers from Ursula to look and act "bourgeois." As a woman with a small child, Ursula didn't need much of a cover. With her cultured background, she had no trouble portraying an executive's wife.

On the long boat ride to Asia, Johann was quite attentive to his "stepson," Michael. Ursula liked that and began falling in love with Johann. On the way to Manchuria, they stopped in Shanghai to pick up supplies and for Rudi to see his son. Ursula asked Rudi to care for Michael overnight so she and Johann could have an overnight trip. Rudi, probably so he could spend some time with his son, agreed to give his wife and her boyfriend a night together.

Soon thereafter, Ursula, Johann, and young Michael traveled to Manchuria. However, Johann returned to Shanghai to buy transformers for the clandestine radio while Ursula looked for a house to rent. Ursula found what we call today a "mother-in-law" cottage tucked behind a much larger house. The main house on the property was rented by Nazi arms dealer Von Schlewitz. Quite literally, Ursula and her boss/boyfriend would be hiding in plain sight.

In Shanghai, with Rudi's help, Johann secreted the transformers in furniture and successfully shipped them to Manchuria. Soon Ursula was transmitting in Morse code to Russian operatives. While Ursula handled the communications, Johann made bombs to be smuggled to their various operatives. In January 1935, Rudi joined them for a while. He brought needed parts and enjoyed spending time with his four-year-old son.

The stress of living a clandestine life and being a mom to an active four-year-old took a toll on Ursula. She lost considerable weight. On at least one occasion, Von Schelwitz invited Ursula to dinner at his home. It is telling he didn't also invite Johann. Hoping to gather some intelligence, Ursula flirted with Von Schelwitz, but nothing came of her efforts. Over dinner, Von Schelwitz also tried, unsuccessfully, to learn more about his renter's background.

While Ursula did not divulge any secrets, she did share with Von Schelewitz her feelings of dread, how she feared that something terrible would happen. Even though Von Schelwitz was a Nazi sympathizer, Ursula asked him to take of her son if something happened to her (and presumably Johann). Von Schelewitz agreed.

After informing Moscow that one of her key operatives had been arrested by the Kempai, the Japanese equivalent of the Gestapo, Ursula and Johann were ordered to leave Manchuria and set up operations in Peking. However, in Peking, Ursula and Johann didn't get any specific orders. They were essentially tourists. While in Peking, Ursula learned she was pregnant. She did not tell Johann or Moscow of the pregnancy.

Ursula returned to Shanghai and told Rudi she was pregnant with Johann's child. He urged her to have an abortion. Johann later made the same request. However, Ursula wanted to keep the child, and besides, abortions were illegal in China.

Rudi wanted to be a spy like his wife and joined the clandestine communist effort. Unaware that Ursula was pregnant and apparently unaware of her romantic involvement with Johann, Rudi and Ursula received orders to set up covert operations in Poland.

On the way to Poland, Ursula and her family stopped in the UK, where much of Ursula's family, including the beloved nanny, Olga, had settled. In part, because she spoke little English, Olga was not happy in England. Further, she felt rather useless, there were no children for her to mother. Olga volunteered to help Ursula care for the children in Poland. While in Poland, Ursula gave birth to a daughter named Janina. Olga, then aged fifty-five, doted on the baby. She was less fond of Michael.

Ursula's work in Poland was fairly routine. She relayed radio messages from Moscow to operatives in the field and back. In one radio message, she learned she had been awarded the Order of the Red Banner, Russia's highest military honor. Before she returned to Moscow to be officially decorated, Ursula, Olga, Rudi, and the children went to Czechoslovakia to visit his parents. Rudi told his parents the baby was his. Ursula went on, alone, to Moscow.

Moscow should have been a place of safety for a communist spy, but Stalin was in the middle of one of his many purges. Many of Ursula's friends and comrades, especially foreigners like herself, were being executed or sent to the Gulag. Despite the terror, Ursula remained loyal to the communist cause.

Ursula received new orders to set up a clandestine radio in Geneva—without her husband. In Switzerland, Ursula, the nanny, Olga, and the children made a home in a lovely farmhouse. The view out their door was akin to the opening scene in the *Sound Of Music*. Michael, now seven, tobogganed to school. The family made friends with neighbors and other foreigners. No doubt some were spies like themselves. Olga and Ursula clashed occasionally about the children. Olga felt she was the better mother and often referred to Nina as "my child."

When she was first recruited as a spy, Richard Sorge had been Ursula's boss and her lover. In Manchuria, her lover, Johann Petra, technically was her boss, but theirs was a true working partnership. In Switzerland, the roles would become fully reversed. Ursula, now a major in the Soviet Army, had two men who reported to her. She would become romantically involved with and marry one of them.

The first man to arrive in Switzerland was Alexander Foote. Unlike the other men in Ursula's life, Foote was apolitical. He was simply a man of adventure. Foote found Ursula pleasant and attractive; their relationship remained professional. Ursula directed Foote to travel on a tourist visa to Munich and wait for further instructions. The second man, Len Beurton, felt attracted to Ursula right away. However, she was disinterested. Ursula dispatched Len to Frankfort.

While Foote and Beurton were in German, Petra came for a quick visit but was not particularly attentive to his daughter or Michael. This annoyed Ursula. Rudi also came for a short visit. He then departed for Shanghai to be a spy himself. His new boss would be no other than Richard Sorge, his wife's former lover.

In Germany, the violence against Jews kept escalating. Jewish-owned businesses were ransacked regularly, and Jews stripped of their German citizenship. Stripped of her citizenship, Ursula could not renew her passport. She was a communist working for the Soviet Union but considered herself German.

Her operative, Alexander Foote, learned that Hitler regularly dined at a certain restaurant. By radio and using code, he advised bombing the restaurant to assassinate Hitler. Foote and Beurton returned to Switzerland to finalize plans with Ursula to kill Hitler. Ursula radioed Moscow for approval and soon received money for bomb-making and other expenses.

On August 23, 1939, Russia and Germany signed a non-aggression pact. Ursula got orders to cease all clandestine operations against Germany. It was a hard order to obey. If Ursula Kuczynski had defied ordered orders and directed Foote and Beurton to assassinate Hitler, WWII likely could have been prevented.

Ursula's situation in Switzerland was getting precarious and more to the point, Moscow quit sending Ursula money. Further, the Swiss were no longer turning a blind eye to espionage. To avoid being arrested and deported back to Germany, Ursula and the children, as well as Foote and Beurton, needed to get out of Switzerland. As her citizenship had been revoked, Ursula could not renew her passport.

Her handler in Moscow suggested that she and Foote marry. Married to a British citizen, Ursula could get a British passport. Russia was playing the long game; simply providing her with a fake passport would not suffice. Married and living in the UK, Ursula might prove a valuable asset after the war. This would prove to be a very fortuitous decision.

Of course, to marry Foote, Ursula first needed to divorce Rudi. In the legal filing, she needed to state why a divorce should be granted. At Foote's suggestion, Ursula claimed that Rudi had committed adultery with Ursula's sister, Bridgette. (Foote, himself, might have had a brief fling with Bridgette). While Foote would help Ursula commit perjury to help Ursula divorce Rudi, he did not want to enter a sham marriage. Ursula married Len instead.

After marrying Len, Ursula went to the British embassy to get a passport. However, MI-5, British intelligence, had a file on her new husband and had briefly detained Ursula's older brother, Jurgen, as a possible spy—which he was. Still, as a spouse of a British citizen, Ursula got a British passport. With the passport issue resolved, the newlyweds made plans to go to England.

Olga did not want to return to England. Switzerland, she reasoned, was safer. Switzerland was not at war while bombs were regularly dropped on London. Olga felt the children, but especially young Nina, would be safer where they were. Determined to stay in Switzerland with Nina, if not both children, Olga went to the British embassy to report Ursula as a spy. However, with her limited English, a consular officer dismissed her brusquely. Olga told her hairdresser why Ursula was living in lovely and safe Switzerland. The hairdresser informed a Jewish neighbor of Ursula's, and Ursula soon learned of Olga's betrayal.

As a child, Olga was a second mother to Ursula. Her betrayal hurt Ursula deeply. Ursula discussed with her new husband what they should do. If Swiss authorities learned Ursula was a spy, her new British passport wouldn't protect her. Swiss officials would deport Ursula back to Germany. As a Jewish spy, she almost certainly would have been tortured, then killed. Len suggested they shoot Olga, an idea Ursula did not immediately dismiss. However, the new couple made plans to head to England via neutral Spain.

Even with passports, Ursula and Len still needed travel documents. Len was denied the necessary authorization, so Ursula and the children went on to England. Soon Ursula made contact with Soviet intelligence and quickly had another clandestine radio up and running. Moscow paid Ursula fifty-eight British pounds a month for her espionage, a respectable amount of money in wartime England.

Meanwhile, in Switzerland, after providing MI-5 with information about spying operations unrelated to his efforts with Ursula, Len Beurton was issued the necessary papers to travel. In August 1942, Len reunited with his new wife and stepchildren. He also volunteered to join the Royal Air Force, but as he was still high on MI-5's watch list, his orders kept getting "lost." On the bright side, his sham marriage to Ursula was turning into a real one.

Before WWII began, many German citizens were living and working in the UK. One of them was Klaus Fuchs, one of the most brilliant physicists of his time. Fuchs, like the thousands of other Germans in the UK when the war began, was detained. Fuchs was no Nazi, but like Ursula, Fuchs was a dedicated communist. A colleague of Fuchs persuaded British authorities that Fuchs' brain power would be useful to the war effort. The authorities released Fuchs, who began working on Project Maud, the UK's super-secret prelude to the Manhattan Project.

Through an intermediary named Kremer, Fuchs supplied technical information about Project Maud to Ursula's brother, Jurgen. However, for reasons which are not clear, Moscow recalled Kremer. Moscow soon asked Ursula, *not her brother*, to re-recruit Fuchs, and Ursula did so. Like Jurgen and Fuchs, Ursula did not see their actions as a betrayal of their adoptive country. They believed the allies should freely share any technology that could defeat

Hitler. Ursula had another operative named Melita Norwood. Melita provided Ursula with information about British research on non-ferrous metal (metals without iron). Such research was relevant to building an atomic bomb.

Normally, a handler such as Ursula and an operative like Melita would minimize in-person contact. However, Ursula and Melita met regularly for tea. What could be more innocent than two women getting together for tea? Ursula and Melita were hiding in plain sight. Another of Ursula's operatives acquired data on a specialized air-to-ground communication system. With the help of this operative, Ursula planted communists into an American-led operation to parachute anti-Nazi Germans behind enemy lines.

Fuchs remained, by far, the most important operative. Fuchs was one of a relatively small number of physicists who understood the underlying mathematics and physics involved in building an atomic bomb. From 1941 to 1943, Fuchs supplied Agent Sonya with over five hundred pages of technical reports, schematic drawings, and designs for uranium enrichment. Technical material, such as schematic drawings, could not be communicated to Moscow by radio. To get this information to Moscow, Ursula relied on the standard practice of dead drops and brush contacts. Often Ursula bicycled her way to the rendezvous. With gasoline rationing, traveling by bicycle was quite common. Again, Ursula was hiding in plain sight. For her efforts, Ursula received a promotion to colonel.

The Allied atomic bomb had to be built in the United States, out of the reach of German bombs. The Americans would dub the effort to build an allied atomic bomb, The Manhattan Project. Fuchs' noble-prize brainpower was needed in America. Before he left, Ursula arranged for Fuchs to have a new handler in the US.

During the war, MI-5 was very adept at catching German spies and many were turned into double agents. Their ability to decode the infamous German Enigma was documented in the Oscar awarding winning moving the *Imitation Game* and elsewhere. However, British intelligence had little success ferreting out Soviet spies. As noted, they had an extensive file on Ursula's husband. An investigator named Roger Willis twice questioned Ursula at her home. Willis concluded Ursula was simply a dutiful wife and mother. Because the clues to Ursula's complicity were so obvious, some have speculated that Willis was a Soviet operative, but the more likely explanation is that his belief system was so ingrained that he simply could not fathom a mother with children being a major spy.

Millicent Bagot, the highest-ranking woman in British intelligence, firmly believed that Ursula was a spy. However, her boss, Roger Willis, overruled her. Had Bagot gone over Willis' head to his boss, Kim Philby, she would likely have been told to accept Willis's judgment, not because he didn't believe in her judgment, but rather because Philby was a double agent working for Moscow.

On September 8, 1943, Ursula gave birth to a boy she named Peter. Shortly thereafter, her new husband received authorization to serve in the RAF, but was never given a position of any importance. With her husband living on base, Ursula became, on a practical basis, a single mother of three children: Michael, Nina, and Peter.

It was common practice at the time for Brits, who could afford the fees, to send their children to boarding schools. In part, because she was afraid her son would discover the clandestine radio, she put Peter in a boarding school. Nine-year-old Nina also went to a boarding school, but Ursula quickly brought her back home.

Ursula did not know it then, but her first husband, Rudi, had been arrested in Iran for spying. Rudi spent several days in detention before being handed over to the Soviets. Rudi's political allegiance, however, was considered suspicious. He was sentenced to five years in the Gulag. The Japanese arrested Johann, Ursula's lover in Manchuria. He was tortured and then executed.

Alexander Foote fared better. At the end of the war, he admitted to British authorities that he had spied for the Soviet Union. The government detained him, but as he had spied for an ally, the Soviet Union MI-5 let him go. Alexander revealed many secrets to British integrators, but like Johann, he did not snitch on Ursula. After his release, he made his way to Paris. The Soviets recruited him, but he became a double agent for the British.

On August 6, an atomic bomb was dropped on Hiroshima and three days later a second bond was dropped on Nagasaki. The United States was the only country with the bomb. American factories, bridges, railroads, and ports, unlike in Europe and Japan, were fully operational. With its industrial strength and America being the only atomic power, a Pax America existed. The Pax America was expected to last for many years, if not decades. All that shattered when, on August 29, 1949, the Soviet Union tested its first atomic bomb. The information that Fuchs provided Ursula, which she forwarded to the Soviet Union, cut years of production time and saved millions of rubles in development costs.

On February 3, 1950, Fuchs was arrested. Ursula learned of his arrest in her daily newspaper. Under interrogation, Fuchs quickly admitted his role. He implicated an American couple, Julius and Ethel Rosenberg, as co-conspirators. Tried in an American court, Julius and Ethel Rosenberg were convicted of treason.

Ethel Rosenberg, however, was no Agent Sonya. Her involvement in espionage was mainly clerical, typing up reports for her husband. As her actions were primarily clerical, some called for mercy, but she and her husband both were sentenced to death. Julius and Ethel were executed by the electric chair on June 19, 1953. Ethel's execution went poorly, and additional shocks were needed.

What Fuchs told investigators about her role; Ursula could only guess. She had to fear the worst. Still, leaving England would be a hard decision. Her eldest son Michael had a scholarship to attend college in the upcoming school year. Her daughter Nina was happy in her adoptive country, and England was young Peter's only home. Still, on February 27, 1950, after burying her radio, she and her children left for East Germany. Her husband, Len, joined them in June.

In East Germany, Ursula tried working with East German intelligence but felt that her days involved with espionage were done. She asked to retire, and her resignation was accepted. Ursula went on to write fourteen books of historical fiction.

In 1953, Rudi was released from the Gulag. Two years later, he made his way to Berlin. Father and son reunited after sixteen years of separation. Both remained in East Germany. Rudi died in 1997. He had lived long enough to see Germany reunited.

Nina's father, Johann, had settled in Brazil and married. In January 1978, he had an emotional reunion with Ursula. He returned to Brazil without seeing his daughter. Johann died in 1977.

Also, in 1977, Ursula went to the UK to promote her autobiography, *Sonya's Report*. Traveling to the UK, Ursula risked being arrested for espionage. However, MI-5 did not want the ineptitude of Willis and the others exposed. The disclosure that Kim Philby had worked for decades as a double agent still stung. It was in MI-5's interest not to arrest Ursula for her spying activities over three decades ago.

Ursula's husband, Len Beurton, suffered from bouts of depression and longed to return to England. He died in 1997.

Ursula died in 2000 at the age of ninety-three. As with the other women profiled in this book, she was a woman of great importance.

The History of This Book

In May 2019, while on vacation in Key West, my wife and I stopped at the History of Diving Museum. The museum's collection includes a collection of diving helmets from around the world, a replica of the first diving bell, and various other memorabilia. There is also a small auditorium where local experts give lectures.

One of the most impressive exhibits, showing on a continuous twenty-minute loop, is the first movie with underwater scenes, a silent picture, *Terrors of the Deep*. This short movie, based on Jules Verne's classic *20,000 Leagues under the Sea,* was filmed in 1914, decades before the invention of scuba. While comical by modern standards, for its time, *Terrors of the Deep* was a technical triumph.

A nearby placard explained that the movie was filmed by John Ernest (J.E.) Williamson and his then-girlfriend. Lilah Freeland Williams. As husband and wife, J.E. and Lilah went on to make several underwater movies. Their technical skill in underwater filmmaking was unsurpassed. I left the museum with a vague idea of writing a book. The lives of J.E. and Lilah Williamson barely merit a Wikipedia entry. They are the most minor of historical figures.

Like everyone else, I was familiar with the life of Amelia Earhart. One part of her life fascinated me. In Amelia Earhart's time, a woman did not travel around the world with a man who was not her husband. Amelia did so with the support of her husband. Countless books have been written about Amelie Earhart and other Big Women of history. But what about the Lilah Williamsons? Moreover, what about the men in their lives? Who were their George Putnams to their Amelia Earharts?

After my wife and I returned to our native California, I completed the final edits of my first book, *In Place of the Parent: Inside Child Protective Services,* and worked on rough drafts of my second book, *Build A Better Bridge: Social Policy for the 21st century. In Place of the Parent* was published in 2020. *Build A Better Bridge* came out in February 2022.

In the summer of 2022, through a Facebook writers' group, I connected with my future editor, Cherime MacFarlane. In February 2023, we signed a contract for her to publish *Beyond Amelia: Lesser-known Women of History.*

In print format, over 500,000 new books are published each year, and another 500,000 are published in digital format only. Favorable reviews are critical for a book to be a commercial success. If you enjoyed *Beyond Amelia,* please post a review. (I have it on good authority that bad karma comes to those who write negative reviews).

For links to my first two books and links to podcast interviews, please visit *lancehillsinger.net*

For more information about the History of Diving Museum, visit their website, divingmuseum.org.

Notes

Introduction:

An ancient alabaster art piece depicts Enheduanna performing a ritual with three male attendants *assisting*.

Fred Noonan married his second wife shortly before his flight with Amelia. He had no children from his first wife. In yesteryear, many gay men entered into sham marriages. Some have speculated that Noonan was one of those men. If Fred was gay, that might explain why George was willing to let his wife travel around the world with Fred.

When Amelia Earhart was ten years old, her father tried to get her to take a ride in a biplane, but perhaps, sensing that aviation safety was still in its infancy, she demurred.

George Putman, the husband of Amelia Earhart, should not be confused with George Putnam, the broadcaster. (Some believe that Ted, the newscaster on the *Mary Tyler Moore Show*, was patterned after George Putnam, the broadcaster. *The Mary Type Moore* show, in a comedic way, often dealt with sexism in the workplace).

Adventurers:

Introduction:

Technically, Queen Teuta was not a pirate. She was the sovereign of Illyria and fought against Roman domination. However, Rome considered her a pirate.

The only surviving contemporaneous account of pirates is a 1724 work by an unknown author titled, *A General History of the Robberies and Murders of the most notorious Pyrates*. Historians agree that the "*General History* of Pyrates" has many inaccuracies, errors, and embellishments.

Mary's paternal grandmother may not have been as naïve as most have suggested. The loss of a child would have been "village news." Mary's "grandmother" *may* have known the truth, but to avoid scandal, went along with the ruse.

Ann Bonny and Mary Read

Plunder included gold, silver, jewelry, furs, foodstuffs, and, of course, beer. Beer, because of its alcoholic content, keeps better than fresh water.

There was one benefit of serving in the British Navy—the daily rum ration, a practice that continued until 1970.

Unique to the Caribbean and the Atlantic seaboard was the pirate flag of skull and crossbones. The pirate flag was flown to intimidate, and the ploy often worked. To confuse their intentions, pirates sometimes would fly a national flag.

Colin Woodard, the author of The Republic of Pirates, states that Anne Bonny "cuckolded" her husband, James Bonny. Technically, a "cuckold" enjoys his wife's sexual prowess with another man. Calling James Bonny hen-pecked would have been a more accurate term.

Zheng Li Sao

There are other spellings of Zheng Li Sao.

Nellie Bly and Elizabeth Bisland

Telegraph service to Asia did not exist until 1902, so reports of the women's travels went by mail.

Ruth Law

Ruth also flew commercial flights, but she is best known for her solo flying. There are differing accounts of the grapefruit story.

Charles may not have been as chauvinistic as it seems. Surely, over the years, he and Ruth discussed her eventual retirement.

Gertrude Bell

The desert can also be quite cold. In January 1918, the city of Ha'il, where Gertrude was held hostage, had a record low of -7 degrees Fahrenheit.

Historians use the term "British" loosely. The United Kingdom (the UK) comprises England, Wales, Scotland, and Northern Ireland. However, in common usage, British interests are synonymous with the interests of the UK.

T.H. Lawrence died in a motorcycle accident in England on May 19, 1935.

France, which originally built the Suez Canal, retained a large minority interest.

The photo taken in front of the pyramid was cropped to show Churchill, Lawrence, and Bell together. In the original photo, many other dignitaries were present.

Gertrude Bell also had a hand in the 1917 Balfour Declaration. A declaration that stated Israel was to be *a* home for Jews. An earlier draft had read that Israel was to be *the* home for Jews. The less restrictive text recognized that mostly Muslims inhabited the land of what was then called Palestine.

Behind the Throne:

Introduction:

Several Roman emperors adopted middle-aged men as a son. This allowed, more or less, a smooth transition of power when the emperor died.

In the Ottoman Empire, caliphs often had multiple wives and concubines. Over the centuries, the power and legitimacy of caliphs waxed and waned, but unlike in medieval Europe, there was never a shortage of male heirs.

Boudica

Granting land to retiring soldiers in occupied territories instead of the Italian peninsula kept experienced troops away from the seat of power and lessened the chance of a coup.

Augustus, the most famous Roman emperor, ordered that so long as the Jews paid their taxes, they should be allowed to worship as they pleased. Suetonius would have been wise to show the same respect for the Druid religion.

If, indeed, slaves raped the daughters, your author speculates that Decianus would have first offered the "opportunity" to his officers. The officers, realizing that the locals would exact retribution, declined.

Why were there more women than men following Boudica? It is hard to know for sure. More men than women might have believed that rebelling against Rome was a lost cause, or women might have felt more comfortable with a female leading the charge.

Historical records are unclear about where Pastogaus was during the battle of Mona. Your author speculates he might have been murdered outside of the battle because Rome wanted to suppress the contents of the will.

The Roman Empire obtained much of its grain from Egypt. Having another source of grain, in case of rebellion in Egypt or a bad harvest, was a prudent policy.

Toregene and Fatima

It is probably more accurate to say that the one percent figure represents the descendants of Genghis Khan *and the Mongol soldiers* under his command.

Some sources say that the taxation plan was implemented by Ogodei. However, as Toregene managed the day-to-day finances of the empire, it was likely was her idea to impose taxation to supplement irregular income from booty.

Roxelena (aka Hurrem)

The exact date of Hurrem's marriage to Sulieman is not known. It might have been in 1523.

An episode of Josh Gates' TV show *Expedition Unknown* focused on the search for Sulieman's heart.

Empress Dowager Cixi

Twenty-one of the captured diplomats perished. They had been bound tightly with ropes. Periodically, to increase tension, water was added to the ropes. It was an excruciating, painful way to die. The Chinese referred to such execution method as "death by a thousand cuts."

One member of the Board of Regents was sent to an obscure post.

The Wade-Giles system was in use until the communists took over. The communist ordered different accent marks be used. Perhaps to reflect revolutionary zeal, these accent marks are referred to as "radicals."

Frederic Ward died in battle. A British Officer, Charles Gordon, took over the command. To the consternation of many Chinese, Cixi was publicly and lavishly praised by Gordon. As noted, xenophobia can cut both ways.

Today, "reverse harem," when a woman has many male relationships, is a sub-genre of fictional literature.

The main qualification for Longyu to be appointed Empress Dowager and for Zaifeng to act as regent apparently was that they would not be sell-outs to Japan. Still, there must have been others that Cixi could have, and perhaps should have, used.

Puyi would become known as the Last Emperor of China. His life story is depicted in the movie of the same name.

Mary Bethune

Albert went on to become a funeral home director.

In 1931, Mary's school merged with Cookman College, and the school became a community college. Mary was elected as college President.

During the Great Depression, while millions of men lost their jobs, the number of women working increased.

In 1942, with WWII raging, the New Deal Programs were phased out. The NYA was transferred to the War Manpower Commission.

Seanelle Hawkins has a Ph.D. in education, so some writers refer to her as Dr. Hawkins. However, according to style guides, outside of academic settings, only those with medical degrees should be referred to as "Dr."

Entrepreneurs:

Introduction:

Deed restrictions often prohibited African-American men or women from buying real estate. This discrimination is one aspect of the controversial Critical Race Theory. The importance of homeownership and the ability to pass wealth down to the next generation is a theme in my second book, *Build A Better Bridge: Social Policy for the 21st Century*.

Women now outnumber men in college 11 to 7.

Until the early 20th century, most secretaries were men.

In 1906, because of the proliferation of "cure-all" tonics, creams, and questionable medical devices, the FDA was created.

Madame Tussaud

In preindustrial times, barbers doubled as doctors. The traditional barber pole, with its red (for blood) and white (for bandages) initially indicated that the shopkeeper was both a barber and a doctor.

Martha Matilda Harper

The increase in automation, the decline of the US's share of the world economy, and other market forces, like the sharp decline in owner-operated single-sex barbershops and hair salons, are discussed in my second book, *Build a Better Bridge: Social Policy for the 21st Century*.

Marie Laveau

In the 21st century, a woman can legally make decent money as a cam-girl or a stripper. Such vocations, with rare exceptions, are not available to men. Of course, most women (and most men) would find working in a sex-related vocation morally repugnant. Encouraging moral behavior in men and women is a sub-topic in *Build a Better Bridge: Social Policy for the 20th Century*.

Mary Goddard

Congress banned debtors' prisons in 1833.

One representative, Thomas McKean, signed after the others. His name was not included in Mary's printing.

Some sources say Belinda Sterling was a slave and freed upon Mary's death. Whether a slave or a freewoman, your author could not find any reference regarding what Belinda Sterling did with her inheritance.

Scientists and Scholars:

Introduction:

In imperial China, bureaucrats, known as Mandarins, collected taxes, administered laws, etc. When an emperor was weak, which was often the case, mandarins set policy and ran the government.

As so many men died in WWI, in France, by the 1930s, women were the majority of graduate students in physics.

Literacy rates are typically calculated for those aged fifteen and up.

Fatima al-Samarqandi

Fatima is the name of Muhammed's wife and remains a popular girl's name in the Muslim world.

Likely due to the history of widespread illiteracy, oral tradition is strong in Muslim culture. Even today, there are literate Muslims who can recite the entire Koran by rote.

Henrietta Leavitt

The distance to nearby stars can be calculated with the parallax method. The parallax method has been used for centuries to calculate distances on earth.

Heddy Lamar

At a showing of *Ecstasy*, Fritz socialized with Hitler and Mussolini, but Fritz was half-Jewish and, not surprisingly, soon had a falling out with the Nazis.

Heddy and Antheil were unaware of the problems with torpedoes. It was important to keep such a design flaw secret from the enemy.

Markey was proud, some would say vain, about his military service. Even after he retired from the navy to all but his closest friends, he insisted on being addressed as admiral.

Spies:

Introduction:

The most decorated spy, male or female, in WWII, was Odette Samson. During the war, Odette fell in love and married a fellow spy named Peter Churchill. When she and Peter were captured, she duped the Germans into believing she and Peter were married and that Peter was a cousin of Prime Minister Winston Churchill. The ruse worked, likely saving both of their lives, and kept Peter, but not Odette, from being tortured. Odette and Peter married, for real, after the war, but the marriage did not last.

Elizabeth Van Lew and Mary Bowser

Some sources say that the Van Lews baptized other slaves in their church.

Louise Marie Bettignies

Louise also asked her mother about becoming a spy.

The Order of the British Empire medal has five classifications. Marie received the fourth most prestigious classification. If she had been a man, she likely would have received a more prestigious classification.

Clara Immerwhar

In 1933, German authorities told Fritz to fire anyone on his staff that was Jewish. He refused to do so and fled to England. However, as the "father of chemical warfare," Fritz wasn't much welcomed. He died of a heart attack while driving to Italy.

Clara and Fritz's son, Herman, committed suicide shortly after WWII.

Aline Griffith

For clarity, events in Aline's life are not necessarily given chronologically.

Ursula Kuczynski

Ursula later took on a third subordinate, an older man named Franz Obermann.

Despite the war, Danish and Noble-winning physicist Niels Bohr was able to write to colleagues in England. In one letter, he said, "Give my regards to Maud." Aware that the Nazis likely read Bohr's mail, British intelligence believed "Maud" was a code word. Maud, however, was the housekeeper Bohr had when he lived in England as a child. Once they realized the error, the British thought Maud made an excellent code word for their new secret project.

This author speculates that Kremer's loyalties might have been suspect. Moscow might have seen Ursula as more reliable.

Klaus Fuchs served nine years in prison, was deprived of British citizenship, and, after serving his sentence, was deported to East Germany.

Aline Griffith

Mount Saint Vincent is now coeducational, with 72% of enrollment female.

Other sources say Aline's father worked as an insurance salesman. Whatever the case, the family was apparently middle-class.

Mr. Tomlinson was undoubtedly an alias.

The CIA and the FBI still train at the farm.

As Spain was neutral, it was allowed to ship equal amounts of oil to both sides. The State Department, as noted, was charged with monitoring compliance.

REFERENCES

Note:

Web pages are frequently updated. The links were valid when the manuscript was being finalized.

ADVENTURERS

Introduction

https://www.familytree.com/blog/privateers-during-the-war-of-1812/

Anne Bonny and Mary Read

https://dloc.com/AA00064190/00001

http://www.thewayofthepirates.com/famous-pirates/mary-read/

https://www.postandcourier.com/news/the-true-and-false-stories-of-anne-bonny-pirate-woman-of-the-caribbean/article_e7fc1e2c-101d-11e8-90b7-9fdf20ba62f8.html

Woodward, C. The Republic Of Pirates Being the True and Surprising Story of the Carribbean Pirates and the Man that Brought them Down. Harcourt. (2007).

https://www.postandcourier.com/news/a-22-year-old-youtuber-may-have-solved-anne-bonny-pirate-mystery-300-years-after/article_78fc0a2e-2914-11eb-a5f5-03b65f4d281a.html

Zheng Yi Sao

https://www.qaronline.org/blog/2020-06-20/pirate-profile-cheng-i-sao

https://daily.jstor.org/cheng-i-sao-female-pirate/

https://en.wikipedia.org/wiki/Zheng_Yi_Sao

http://www.thewayofthepirates.com/famous-pirates/ching-shih/

http://www.cindyvallar.com/ZhengYiSao.html

https://www.history.com/topics/british-history/spanish-armada#

Nellie Bly and Elizabeth Bisland

https://wams.nyhistory.org/modernizing-america/modern-womanhood/nellie-bly/

https://www.womenshistory.org/education-resources/biographies/nellie-bly

https://www.theguardian.com/lifeandstyle/2021/jun/24/mystery-of-wheelie-suitcase-how-gender-stereotypes-held-back-history-of-invention

https://publicdomainreview.org/essay/elizabeth-bislands-race-around-the-world

https://marshallmgoldberg.com/2014/12/competitor-emerges/

Ruth Law

https://en.wikipedia.org/wiki/Ruth_Law

https://www.smithsonianmag.com/smithsonian-institution/ace-aviatrix-learned-fly-even-though-orville-wright-refused-teach-her-180962606/

https://www.ctie.monash.edu/hargrave/law.html

Gertrude Bell

https://www.biography.com/news/gertrude-bell-biography-facts

https://www.historic-uk.com/HistoryUK/HistoryofBritain/Gertrude-Bell/

BEING ON (OR BEHIND) THE THRONE:

Boudica

https://www.historic-uk.com/HistoryUK/HistoryofEngland/Boudica/

https://www.historynet.com/boudica-celtic-war-queen-who-challenged-rome.htm

Toregene and Fatima:

https://andrewglockhartwriter.com/2015/11/03/women-behind-the-throne-part-one/

https://www.discovermagazine.com/the-sciences/1-in-200-men-direct-descendants-of-genghis-khan

https://www.worldhistory.org/Ogedei_Khan/

https://www.nationalgeographic.org/article/mongol-khans/

https://www.lonelyplanet.com/mongolia/background/history/00237772

https://andrewglockhartwriter.com/2015/11/03/women-behind-the-throne-part-one/

Roxelena (aka Hurrem)

https://www.britannica.com/biography/Roxelana

https://en.wikipedia.org/wiki/Hurrem_Sultan

https://www.thoughtco.com/suleiman-the-magnificent-195757

https://www.al-monitor.com/originals/2021/05/why-women-are-calling-turkeys-only-female-cabinet-member-resign

Cixi: The Empress Dowager:
https://www.american-rails.com/1840s.html
Empress Dowager Cixi: The Concubine who launched Modern China, Jung Chang, 2013 Anchor Books (a division of Random House) New York 2013.
Mary Bethune:
https://www.womenshistory.org/education-resources/biographies/mary-mcleod-bethune
https://nces.ed.gov/naal/lit_history
https://www.thebalance.com/unemployment-rate-by-year-3305506
Watts, J. *The Black Cabinet: The Untold Story of African Americans and the Politics During the Age of Roosevelt*, Grover Press, New York 2020.
https://nces.ed.gov/naal/lit_history
https://www.thebalance.com/unemployment-rate-by-year-3305506
https://www.historynet.com/boudica-celtic-war-queen-who-challenged-rome.htm

ENTREPENEURS

Eliza Pinckey
https://www.nps.gov/chpi/learn/historyculture/eliza-lucas-pinckney.htm
https://www.womenhistoryblog.com/2008/09/eliza-lucas-pinckney.html
Mary Katherine Goddard:
https://www.womenhistoryblog.com/2016/06/first-women-in-business.html
https://www.smithsonianmag.com/history/mary-katharine-goddard-woman-who-signed-declaration-independence-180970816
https://msa.maryland.gov/msa/educ/exhibits/womenshall/html/goddard.html
Martha Harper
https://www.patentearth.com/blog/the-history-of-koken-barber-chairs.html
https://www.pbs.org/wgbh/theymadeamerica/whomade/harper_hi.html
https://ushistoryscene.com/article/rise-of-public-education/

https://www.atlasobscura.com/articles/martha-matilda-harper-the-greatest-businesswoman-youve-never-heard-of

Mysteries at the Museum, season 13, episode 11, October 12, 2017

Madame Tussaud

https://www.theguardian.com/books/2018/oct/04/madame-tussaud-edward-carey-little

https://www.geriwalton.com/francis-tussaud-madame-tussauds-son/

https://www.goldentours.com/travelblog/facts-about-madame-tussaud-museum

https://www.lego.com/en-us/aboutus/lego-group/management

Marie Laveau

https://ghostcitytours.com/new-orleans/marie-laveau/

https://www.womenhistoryblog.com/2012/07/marie-laveau.html

https://64parishes.org/entry/free-people-of-color

https://www.justice.gov/usao-ndca/us-v-elizabeth-holmes

https://www.npr.org/2022/11/23/1138477784/elizabeth-holmes-sentenced-11-years-explained

https://www.jbhe.com/news_views/51_gendergap_universities.html

SCHOLARS AND SCIENTISTS:

Introduction:

https://egscholars.com/2021/12/21/top-5-least-educated-countries-in-africa

https://www.american.edu/cas/economics/ejournal/upload/grande_accessible.pdf

Hypatia

https://www.smithsonianmag.com/history/hypatia-ancient-alexandrias-great-female-scholar-10942888/

https://www.catholicbridge.com/catholic/cyril-hypatia.php

Fatima al-Samarqandi

https://www.dailysabah.com/feature/2015/04/24/fatima-alsamarqandi-an-influential-female-scholar-skilled-calligrapher

https://ibrahimlong.org/2010/08/07/of-love-and-knowledge-the-story-of-fatimah-al-samarqandi/

Emilie Du Chatelet

https://scientificwomen.net/women/du_chatelet-emilie-25

https://plato.stanford.edu/entries/emilie-du-chatelet/
Clara Immerwahr
https://www.bbc.com/news/uk-england-28593256
https://jwa.org/encyclopedia/article/immerwahr-clara
Henritta Leavitt
https://www.famousscientists.org/henrietta-swan-leavitt/
https://www.aavso.org/henrietta-leavitt-%E2%80%93-celebrating-forgotten-astronomer
Heddy Lamar
https://hedylamarr.com/
https://www.womenshistory.org/education-resources/biographies/hedy-lamarr
https://en.wikipedia.org/wiki/Ecstasy_(film)
https://www.electronics-notes.com/articles/history/pioneers/hedy-lamarr-biography-invention.php
https://spartacus-educational.com/2WWusaN.htm
Obama, Barack *A Promised Land*, New York, Crown, 2020

SPIES

Introduction
https://www.biography.com/military-figures/mata-hari
Lydia Barrington Darragh
https://www.womenhistoryblog.com/2010/09/lydia-darragh.html
https://www.ushistory.org/people/darragh.htm
Elizabeth van Lew and Mary Richards
https://encyclopediavirginia.org/entries/van-lew-elizabeth-l-1818-1900/
https://encyclopediavirginia.org/entries/bowser-mary-richards-fl-1846-1867/
https://www.smithsonianmag.com/history/elizabeth-van-lew-an-unlikely-union-spy-158755584/
https://thereconstructionera.com/president-grant-appoints-elizabeth-van-lew-postmaster-for-richmond-gen-longstreet-collector-of-the-port-of-nola-march-1869/

https://www.newworldencyclopedia.org/entry/Mary_Elizabeth_Bowser

https://www.essentialcivilwarcurriculum.com/the-telegraph.html

Louise Marie Bettignies

https://www.history.com/this-day-in-history/battle-of-verdun

https://www.westernfrontassociation.com/on-this-day/27-september-1918-louise-de-bettignies-alias-alice-dubois-died-on-this-day/

https://www.encyclopedia.com/women/encyclopedias-almanacs-transcripts-and-maps/de-bettignies-louise-d-1918

http://www.remembrancetrails-northernfrance.com/trails/the-war-of-movement-and-the-first-german-occupation/monument-to-louise-de-bettignies-lille.html

https://www.essentialcivilwarcurriculum.com/the-telegraph.html

https://www.thedailybeast.com/how-the-cia-came-out-of-the-closet

Aliene Griffith

Loftis, L. *The Princess Spy,* Simon and Schuster, New York 2021

https://www.nytimes.com/2017/12/15/obituaries/aline-griffith-model-countess-author-and-spy-is-dead.html

Urusla Kuczynski (aka Agent Sonya)

https://depts.washington.edu/moves/CP_map-votes.shtml

https://www.fbi.gov/history/famous-cases/atom-spy-caserosenbergs

MacIntryre, B. Agent Sonya: *The Spy Next Door* Random House, New York 2021

CONCLUDING REMARKS

https://theconversation.com/hidden-women-of-history-enheduanna-princess-priestess-and-the-worlds-first-known-author

THE HISTORY OF THIS BOOK

https://justpublishingadvice.com/how-many-kindle-ebooks-are-there

www.ingramcontent.com/pod-product-compliance
Lightning Source LLC
Chambersburg PA
CBHW031130160726
47989CB00017B/2526